Reckless

The Story Of Cryptocurrency Interest Rates

Jonathan Bier

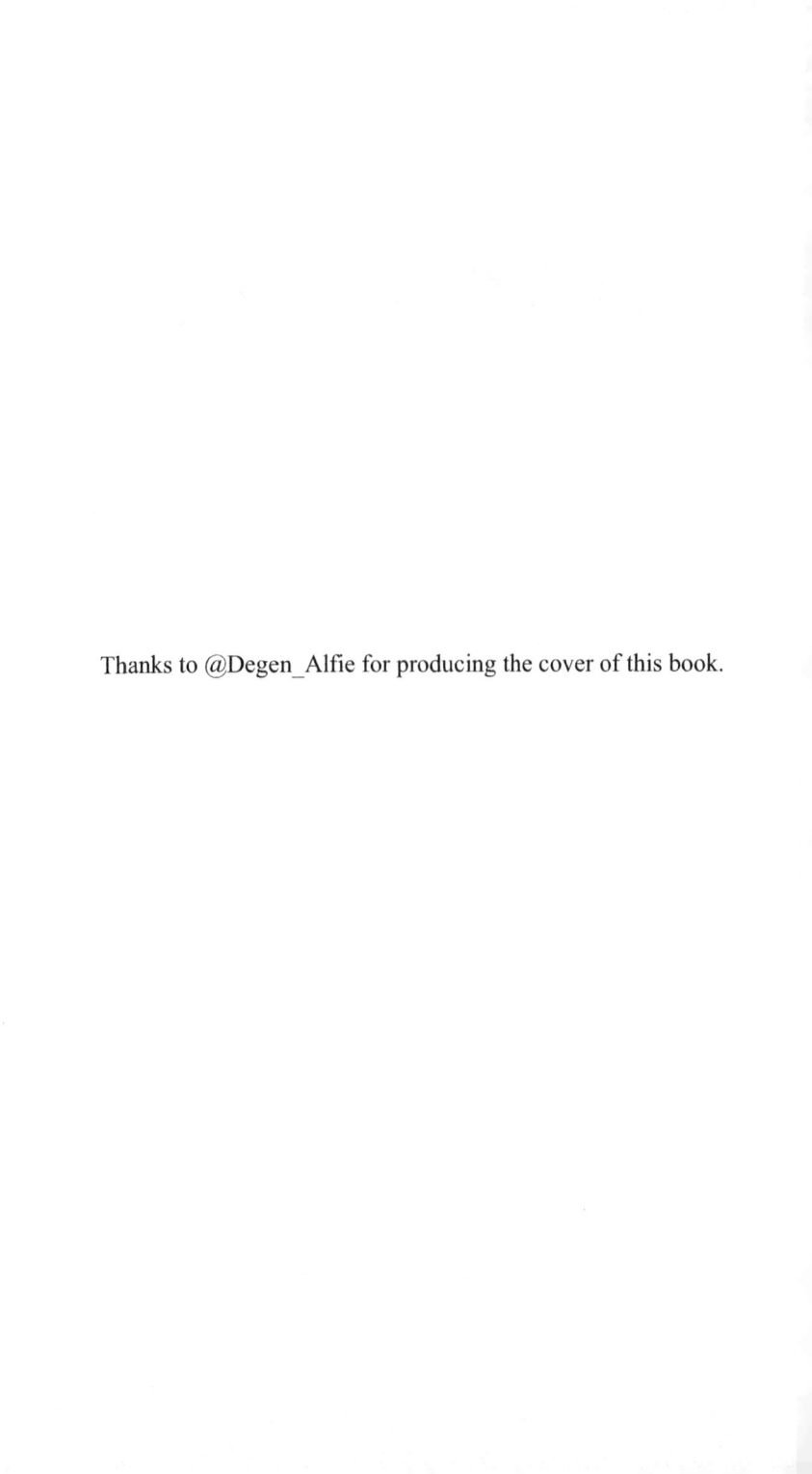

Thanks to @Degen_Alfie for producing the cover of this book.

Introduction

This book begins by providing a brief history of interest rates. It discusses the perplexing conundrum of how to determine the most appropriate base interest rate in an economy. The book then scrutinises conventional wisdom with respect to setting interest rates and considers the potential consequences of rates being set at reckless and inappropriate levels.

The book then moves over to the world of Bitcoin and cryptocurrency, cataloguing various interest rates, quasi-interest rates and different yield structures which have existed throughout the ecosystem's short thirteen year life. The book contrasts some of these structures with those in the world of traditional finance and economics.

The book then explores the emergence of cryptocurrency lending markets, tracking the development and extraordinary growth of these markets into the 2021 yield market bubble. The book disassembles the peculiar components of the cryptocurrency credit market, covering the incestuous relationships between many of the leading lenders and borrowers and the insatiable greed they demonstrated, resulting in the eventual market crash in June 2022.

Finally, in the wake of Ethereum switching to Proof of Stake for its consensus system in late 2022, the book examines the staking yield as a quasi-interest rate, analysing this yield using an economic and financial framework.

Contents

Part One - Interest Rate History

1. The History Of Interest Rates — 2
2. Interest Rate Ethics — 13
3. The Natural Rate — 17
4. The Wrong Rate — 23
5. Everything Bubble — 32
6. Bitcoin Interest Rate — 44

Part Two - Cryptocurrency Interest Rate History

7. The Early Years — 51
8. The Emergence Of Lending Markets — 54
9. Bitcoin As Collateral — 66
10. Bitcoin's Risk Free Rate — 69
11. The Earn Model — 76
12. Stablecoins — 85
13. DeFi — 101
14. Crypto Credit Market Structure — 123
15. Financial Contagion — 137
16. The Earn Collapse — 143
17. Celsius — 157

Part Three - Proof of Stake

18. Proof Of Stake — 174
19. The Proof Of Stake Interest Rate — 180
20. Staking Derivatives — 184
21. Proof Of Stake Economy — 192

Part One

Interest Rate History

The History Of Interest Rates

Ancient Times

Contrary to popular misconceptions, credit and debt are thought to pre-date coinage and money, perhaps by thousands of years.[1] The first records of interest being charged are from Mesopotamia in around 3200 BC, long before coins existed. The written record of interest rate regulation appears to have started in around 1800 BC.[2] Hammurabi, a king of the first dynasty of ancient Babylonia, capped the annual interest rate at 33.3% for grain and 20% for silver. If these limits were found to have been breached, the debt was cancelled.

Ancient Egypt was a largely centralised economy and there are limited records of interest rates in this period. However, a papyrus scroll from 900 BC contains a note that a man received five debens of silver and promises to pay back ten debens in twelve months time, an annual interest rate of 100%. While a tablet from 664 BC records a grain loan at a rate of 75%.[3] In around AD 100, while Egypt was wealthy, interest rates were capped at 12%, while compound interest was banned. Compound interest is when the interest rate not only applies to the principal, but also on accumulated interest charges from previous periods. In Rome in 443 BC, interest rates were capped at 8.33%. This was reduced to 4.17% by 347 BC. Byzantine legal interest rate limits were around 12% in AD 400, before declining to

---
[1] https://www.nakedcapitalism.com/2011/08/what-is-debt-%E2%80%93-an-interview-with-economic-anthropologist-david-graeber.html
[2] A History of Interest Rates by Sidney Homer - Page 3
[3] A History of Interest Rates by Sidney Homer - Page 50

around the 6% to 8% range by AD 700. These limits then appeared to remain stable for several hundred years.

The existence of these limits and regulations indicates that perhaps interest rates and "incorrect" interest rates were already significant enough in scale to cause social, political or economic problems, even thousands of years ago. Therefore regulation may have been demanded as a potential solution. Interest rates seemed to have a cap, perhaps to prevent lenders from exploiting borrowers.

If interest bearing loans were already widespread in ancient Babylonia, perhaps it follows that loans and interest have a long history well before the written record started some 5,000 years ago. Anthropologists and historians tend to believe that interest originated when people lent each other animals or seeds. Animals and seeds are productive assets. Seeds can be used to grow produce, while animals can have offspring. It therefore could make sense that the lender should obtain a share of this growth. We may never know for sure, but this appears to be a reasonable explanation for the origin of interest rates. Therefore, it can be assumed that early interest rates were linked to the growth and the productivity of assets. However, how to determine an appropriate natural interest rate in an economy, remains one of the most controversial and challenging issues in economics and finance, to this day.

Tulip Mania

Often regarded as the first reported financial mania, is the so-called Dutch tulip mania, of the 1630s. This seems particularly appropriate to discuss in this book, given it is about Bitcoin and cryptocurrency and many crypto sceptics often compare the tulip mania to Bitcoin, as a form of criticism. Indeed, the former president of the Dutch Central Bank, Nout Wellink said of Bitcoin:

> *This is worse than the tulip mania, at least then you got a tulip [at the end], now you get nothing.[4]*

The tulip mania is described in Charles Mackay's 1841 book "Extraordinary Popular Delusions and the Madness of Crowds":

> *The rage for possessing them soon caught the middle classes of society, and merchants and shopkeepers, even of moderate means, began to vie with each other in the rarity of these flowers and the preposterous prices they paid for them. A trader at Harlaem was known to pay one-half of his fortune for a single root. So anxious were the speculators to obtain them that one person offered the free-simple of twelve acres of building ground for the Harlaem tulip.*

The book only contains seven pages of coverage on the tulip mania, without significant detail. The book may have elevated the tulip mania as a classic example of a financial bubble, perhaps to that of the most famous financial bubble ever. However there is limited evidence as to the scale or economic impact of the tulip bubble. It is possible that the tulip mania of 1634 is mostly legend and myth. At least, in Mackay's book, its scale is likely to be somewhat exaggerated.

Dutch interest rates during the period are said to have started at around 8% in 1600, before declining to 6.25% by 1620, they then continued their decline to 5% in the 1640s and 4% in the 1650s.[5] Prior to this, from around 1200 to 1500, Dutch rates appear to have been stable for 300 years at around 8%. Dutch interest rates were also considerably lower than in England and other European countries such as France. Rates in England were in the 8% to 10% range in the early 1600s, while French rates were 8%.[6] It is possible these relatively low rates in the Netherlands encouraged an early carry

---

[4] https://www.theguardian.com/technology/2013/dec/04/bitcoin-bubble-tulip-dutch-banker
[5] A History of Interest Rates by Sidney Homer - Page 128
[6] A History of Interest Rates by Sidney Homer - Page 126

trade, borrowing in the Netherlands and investing in England. The only country to have rates as low as the Dutch was Italy, where rates were in the 4% to 6% range from 1300 to 1800. The declining interest rates in the Netherlands could therefore have contributed to the tulip mania, although it is probably fair to say there is insufficient evidence to support this claim, if the tulip mania was even real at all.

Mississippi Scheme

The first chapter in the "Extraordinary Popular Delusions and the Madness of Crowds" covers the Mississippi bubble of 1719. Unlike the tulip mania, it is clear that this bubble, a French one, was real and economically significant. It is also fair to say that artificially low interest rates may have been this bubble's primary cause.

The Mississippi Company was founded in 1684 and held business monopoly trading rights and land claims in the French colonies in North America and the West Indies. The land claims cover approximately 50% of the current United States of America by area. The Mississippi river network can be considered extremely valuable and is probably the largest, most interconnected and powerful river trading transport infrastructure in the world. Shares in the Mississippi Company were made available to the public and in 1719 the stock appreciated in value by 1,900%.

The world "millionaire" is said to have originated to describe the new class of people who benefited from the bubble.[7] These types of widespread, extraordinary and phenomenally fast gains were not seen again for perhaps another 300 years, in the great cryptocurrency bubbles of 2017 and 2021. Except by 2021, it was billionaires, rather than millionaires, which were created.

The unlikely protagonist in the story of this early bubble was a Scottish man, called John Law. In 1694 Law fought a duel in London,

---

[7] DeJean, Joan (2018). Chapter Twelve: The Invention of Money. The Queen's Embroiderer: A True Story of Paris, Lovers, Swindlers and the First Stock Market Crisis

over the affections of a woman called Elizabeth Villiers.[8] Law killed his opponent and was arrested and charged with his murder. He was then found guilty and sentenced to death. With the help of his brother, he managed to get his sentence reduced to a fine before somehow escaping prison and fleeing the country. Despite this dubious past, Law managed to climb the social ladder in France. Louis XIV of France died in 1715 and France's economy was in poor shape, with high debt, shortages of precious metals, deflation and a stagnant economy. This change in administration and the dire economic circumstances provided an opportunity for Law.

Law had a solution to France's economic woes, which was eventually accepted by the new administration in 1716 and Law was appointed the Controller General of Finances, essentially the finance minister. Law's plan was not too dissimilar to the response of central bankers after the global financial crisis in 2008, he was to lower the interest rate and flood the system with new cheap money. This is also said to be the first institutional use of unbacked fiat paper money. The central bank notes were no longer denominated in gold, removing any restriction on the amount of paper that could be issued. Law was free to manipulate the currency in whichever way he saw fit. Free to engage in his plan, Law lowered interest rates to 2% and the money printing machines were operational round the clock, printing larger and larger denominations of paper notes.

Law also took over the Mississippi Company and merged it with France's other trading monopolies in Asia. Then in 1719, the company took over all of France's national debt. Holders of the debt could convert it into Mississippi Company stock. Within just a couple of years, Law had created an extraordinary global financial powerhouse, the largest company in human history. The stock price of the company skyrocketed, it traded at around 50 times earnings, matching the 2% interest rates on which its lofty valuation depended.

---

[8] Adams, Gavin John (2012). Letters to John Law

If one wants an example of a several hundred year old speculative and irrational financial mania in Europe to cynically compare the Bitcoin and the cryptocurrency bubble to, the Mississippi scheme is probably much better suited to that than the tulip mania, which occurred 80 years earlier.

Towards the end of 1719, the huge quantity of money started to produce inflation. Confidence in the paper money began to wane and Law banned the possession of precious metals, because they were seen as a viable alternative to paper money. Law then faced a dilemma, just like the central bankers of 2022, he had to decide whether to keep printing money or let the bubble burst. In 1720 the share price of the Mississippi Company started to collapse and Law was forced to go down the deflationary path. The public rebelled and riots broke out. The central bank was raided and Law's personal property was vandalised. Law resigned as finance minister and then fled the country. This early monetary experiment failed catastrophically, in just a few years.

The Irish/French economist Richard Cantillon, was an early investor in the Mississippi Company, from which he is said to have acquired great wealth. Around ten years after the collapse, in 1730, he wrote a book entitled "Essay on the Nature of Trade in General". His experience as an investor in the Mississippi Company is said to have influenced his thinking. In his book, Cantillon hypothesised that the original recipients of new money enjoy higher standards of living at the expense of later recipients. This observation, that expansion in the money supply doesn't evenly impact everyone at the same time and may actually unfairly increase inequality, is now known as the Cantillon Effect.

Cantillon ended his book with the following paragraph:

> *It is then certain that a bank, in concert with a minister, is able to increase and support the price of public stock and to lower the state's rate of interest with the consent*

of this minister, when these operations are discreetly managed and in this way free the state of its debts. But these refinements, which open the door to making great fortunes, are rarely managed for the sole benefit of the state, and those who operate them are often corrupted. The excessive banknotes that are created and issued on these occasions do not disturb the circulation because, as they are employed for the purchase and sale of capital stock, they are not used for household expenditure and they are not converted into silver. But if some fear or unforeseen accident drove the holders to demand silver at the bank, the bomb would explode, and it would be seen that these are dangerous operations.[9]

Cantillon appears to be indicating that the banks and government can lower interest rates, which can push up the price of financial assets. Many well-connected individuals can then do incredibly well in that environment. The new liquidity is initially trapped in the financial system and not used for "household expenditure". Consumer price inflation can therefore initially remain mild. However, this policy causes imbalances to build up in the economy, which may later result in consumer price inflation, as the trapped liquidity eventually leaks out.

South Sea Bubble

The second chapter of "Extraordinary Popular Delusions and the Madness of Crowds" covers the South Sea bubble in 1720. The British South Sea Company, was founded in 1711. The company had a monopoly to supply African slaves to South America. Just like the Mississippi Company, the company was used to lower the cost of government debt, by allowing investors to convert debt into equity. English interest rates collapsed in the early 1700s from around 8% to 4% by the early 1720s. In a monumental rally, no doubt driven by a

---

[9] https://oll.libertyfund.org/title/essay-on-the-nature-of-trade-in-general-lf-ed

British public who were inspired, captivated and envious of what happened in France, the stock of the company appreciated by nearly 1,000% in the first half of 1720. However, it soon crashed and lost almost all of its gains by the end of the year. As a result, the "Bubble Act"[10] was passed, which banned the formation of public companies, unless approved by royal charter. The law was finally repealed in 1825.

The Great Depression

Perhaps the most significant period, when it comes to influencing the ideologies of the current crop of central bankers and regulators, was the economic crash of 1929 and the great depression which followed it.

The roaring twenties was a period of economic prosperity in the United States. Throughout the twenties interest rates appeared quite reasonable, between 4% and 5%. However, the annual economic growth rate in the period was around 8%, driven by technological innovation. In this context, an interest rate of around half this, can be considered as somewhat low. While consumer prices were stable throughout most of the 1920s, there were signs of unsustainable credit expansion and significant asset price inflation. Property prices in particular, increased considerably. Around 30 skyscrapers per year were completed in Manhattan alone towards the end of the 1920s, compared to around three per year before this period.[11] The Empire State building was famously completed in 1931.[12]

The Dow Jones Industrial average climbed 284% from the start of 1925 to its peak in late 1929, before the stock market crash on 24 October 1929, so-called Black-Thursday. The aftermath of this crash led to the Great Depression, a period of low economic growth from 1929 to 1939.

---

[10] https://books.google.ca/books?id=BYlKAAAAYAAJ
[11] https://buildingtheskyline.org/roaring-twenties/
[12] https://en.wikipedia.org/wiki/Empire_State_Building

Much of the investment in these securities, driving up prices in the bubble period, were credit financed. However, it was not until late 1927 when the market started to lose its link with reality. Prior to this, the rally was matched by strong growth in corporate earnings, driven by new industries such as oil, automotive and electric. In 1927, the Federal Reserve lowered interest rates and increased the purchasing of government securities, following the infamous Long Island meeting. After this, stocks continued to rally even more aggressively, losing the relationship with corporate earnings. This break from reality is an uncomfortable comparison to the everything bubble of 2021. It is easy to say with the benefit of hindsight, however the stock market boom of the late 1920s looked just like another mania. The US president at the time did not seem to agree though. In 1929, when president Calvin Coolidge left office, he said that stocks were "cheap at current levels".[13]

British Economist, John Maynard Keynes, who later became famous for his analysis and diagnosis of the Great Depression, did not appear to spot the bubble early either. In 1928 he said that there was "nothing that can be called inflation yet in sight" and he circulated a note to his friends stating that "stocks would not slump severely."[14] Keynes is said to have lost more than 75% of his net worth in 1929, due to his position in stocks and his portfolio was forced into liquidation. Keynes' fortune of almost £50,000 is said to have been lost. What Keynes failed to see was the scramble for gold in 1929, which forced central banks to tighten policy in order to retain their gold. Keynes famously referred to gold as a "barbarous relic" and believed that without the gold anchor restricting the flexibility of central bank policy, the crash could have been avoided. The Federal Reserve did lower rates to just 1.5% in 1931 as a result of the crash, however Keynes argued it should have done more and that the action it did take was not sufficient.

---

[13] Lords of Finance - Page 314
[14] Lords of Finance - Page 339

While there were only limited signs of consumer price inflation in the 1920s, which could have justified the Federal Reserve tightening, there were signs of excessive credit expansion. Had the Federal Reserve been more focused on these financial conditions, they may not have loosened policy in 1927 and the crisis may have been averted.

The American economist Irving Fisher also lived through the Great Depression. His view, formulated in 1933[15], was that the cause of the depression was Debt Deflation. This situation arises when there is too much debt in the system. Once the debt begins to be paid off, this causes a contraction in the money supply, which leads to deflation. The outstanding debt then becomes more expensive in real terms, which leads to pessimism and hoarding and a continuing downwards spiral. Fisher considered Debt Deflation to be a solvable problem and his solution to the problem was reflation and the stabilisation of the price level. Deflation was considered as a calamitous outcome and something that should be prevented at all costs. Due to the severity of the depression, this mantra became conventional wisdom in modern monetary thinking.

Nobody seemed to agree with Fisher's explanation more than the now Nobel laureate, Ben Bernanke (if you consider economics a "real" Nobel prize that is). Ben Bernanke was the chairman of the Federal Reserve in a key period from 2006 to 2014 and he considered himself somewhat of an expert on the great depression. He even wrote a book on it. The lesson Bernanke took from this was that the Federal Reserve should have been more aggressive in expanding the money supply following the 1929 crash. Indeed, he energetically implemented this idea in the wake of the 2008 crash.

However, like Keynes, Fisher had failed to predict the crash, famously declaring in 1929 that "stock prices had reached what looks like a permanently high plateau".[16]

---

[15] https://fraser.stlouisfed.org/title/debt-deflation-theory-great-depressions-3596
[16] New York Times on October 16, 1929 - Page 8

There is an alternative view on the Great Depression, articulated by members of the Austrian school of economics. Friedrich Hayek, who also lived through the great depression, did not believe all deflation was bad. He distinguished between "good deflation", brought about by technological innovation and "bad deflation", the debt deflation Fisher was concerned about. Hayek and those in the Austrian school believed that rather than avoiding the recession, we should let it run its course. Artificially preventing the recession would allow the imbalances in the economy to persist and malinvestment to continue, prolonging the crisis. Allowing a recession would enable a process of creative destruction, a type of cleansing, where capital and labour could be reallocated to more productive industries. Perhaps dying industries, disrupted by new technology, should be allowed to die? Unlike Fisher and Keynes, Hayek is said to have predicted the 1929 crash.[17] On the other hand, there does not appear to be any clear written record of this prediction, but one can argue his record of predicting the crash is better than Keynes and Fisher. This may only be important if one considers the ability to predict the 1929 crash as relevant when evaluating their analysis of the causes of it, after the event.

Regardless of the merits of either side of the debate, the Keynes/Fisher interpretation became conventional wisdom, while the Austrian interpretation was ignored by mainstream economists and politicians. It was considered vital to prevent deflation at all costs and lowering the interest rate was the key tool available to achieve this objective.

---

[17] https://www.nobelprize.org/prizes/economic-sciences/1974/press-release/

2

Interest Rate Ethics

The legitimacy and ethics of interest has long been a contentious issue. Famously under Islamic finance, interest is typically banned. The term usury, which means interest on loans at an unreasonably high level, is associated with unethical lending, enriching the lender at the expense of the borrower. It is not only in Islam. Perhaps less well known is that Jewish/Christian bible also has texts which look unfavourably on interest.

> *You shall not charge interest on loans to your brother, interest on money, interest on food, interest on anything that is lent for interest.*[18]

While in historical Jewish, Christian or Islamic societies, interest of any kind was considered wrong, in other societies, including today, interest is considered ok as long as the rates are not deemed exploitative. Interest rates above a certain level are often regulated or seen as unethical and unfair.

In 1849, perhaps the first person to declare himself an anarchist, French philosopher Pierre-Joseph Proudhon argued against the legitimacy and efficacy of interest, in a discussion with another French economist, Bastiat.

---

[18] Deuteronomy 23:19

> *[Interest constitutes] a reward for idleness, [and is] the basic cause for inequality, but also of poverty. I call interest theft.*[19]

Proudhon went on to criticise the exponential growth implicit in compound interest, which could lead to unsustainable debt burdens that could cripple the economy and lead to stagnation. In theory, compound interest can keep enlarging the debt burden, such that the amount of debt exceeds the total amount of money in the world. This theory has grown increasingly popular in the aftermath of the 2008 global financial crisis. For example, this theory is explained in the 2011 movie "Zeitgeist: Moving Forward", which has over 25 million YouTube views.[20] This film argues that modern money is based on debt and with the impact of compounding interest, repaying all the debt is mathematically impossible and therefore the economy must become more and more indebted until we have stagnation and then the system collapses.

Proudhon also argued that interest fuels antagonism between the lenders and the borrowers. Proudhon advocated lowering interest rates to near zero, plus introducing a wealth tax, such that the effective interest rate would be negative.[21] This, Proudhon argued, would result in an economic boom, with no bankruptcies, higher consumption and guaranteed employment. Such an experiment was never carried out in society, except perhaps until 2009 when interest rates went to near zero and bonds started trading at negative rates. Proudhon would have been delighted.

The liberal economist Bastiat countered Proudhon by arguing that interest was a fair price for a mutually agreed exchange of services. The lender provides use of his/her capital for a period of time and time has value. Instead of depressing output, interest encourages lenders to provide capital, which boosts production, benefiting all. If there were no interest rates, why would anyone lend? You could have

---
[19] https://www.idler.co.uk/article/book-of-the-week-the-price-of-time/
[20] https://www.youtube.com/watch?v=4Z9WVZddH9w&t=4274s
[21] The Price of Time - Page xviii

a "People's Bank" that could lend. However, in a lesson similar to the one Richard Cantillon learned over one hundred years earlier during the Mississippi scheme, a centralised system distributing newly issued money is not likely to be able to allocate these funds equally to everyone in a fair manner. It may result in a system where only the wealthy and well connected can borrow. The poor may be unable to borrow, trapped on the wrong side of an interest rate apartheid.

At least one early Bitcoiner appears to have been an admirer of Proudhon. In early 2011 a user on the BitcoinTalk forum, with the username "Proudhon" began enthusiastically talking about his Bitcoin mining operations.[22] This Proudhon never appeared to be a massive fan of speculation and Bitcoin price appreciation, he seemed to mostly want to mine Bitcoin and use Bitcoin as decentralised money. Just hoping for the price to go up was laziness, a "reward for idleness" and this is an aspect of Bitcoin Proudhon appeared to dislike. After the June 2011 Bitcoin price crash, Proudhon became quite negative on Bitcoin and the Bitcoin price. In December 2011, when the Bitcoin price was around US$2.50, Proudhon wrote:

> *Did anyone sincerely believe any significant amount of new money was entering this pathetic system? It's just old money changing hands, and as I've said before, you can't get the price to stick in that kind of scenario. It'll bounce around after large drops and might recover to nearly the "stable" pre-drop price, but, ultimately, the price will continue going down as long as no new money enters the system; and, again, it's apparent that there isn't really any new money entering the system and there's absolutely no reason for anyone to put money into this sinking ship.*[23]

Proudhon then continued his negativity and scepticism into the next Bitcoin price bubble in 2013. In a timely post, right before the

---
[22] https://bitcointalk.org/index.php?topic=3889.msg90005#msg90005
[23] https://bitcointalk.org/index.php?action=profile;u=9636;sa=showPosts;start=3920

monumental April 2013 Bitcoin price crash, a parody song was published, "The Proudhon Song". This parody of Proudhon's negative views is to the tune of "Girl on Fire" by Alicia Keys:

> *Bitcoin's a fad and it's on fire.*
> *Higher than a fantasy, like a singularity.*
> *Bulls are living in a world full of denial.*
> *I'm feeling a catastrophe, they're thinking it can fly away.*
> *I keep on riding my bear, though I'm falling a tear.*
> *It's gonna crash to the ground and I'm not backing down.*
> *Bitcoin is a bubble...*
> *Bitcoin is a bubble...*[24]

---

[24] https://www.youtube.com/watch?v=A7TuFy0fcuw

3

The Natural Rate

There is a concept in economics called the natural rate of interest, which is sometimes called the equilibrium rate. This rate is considered the most appropriate rate, some kind of fair equilibrium interest rate, which maximises the utilisation of available resources in the economy. This rate can therefore be considered as an optimal rate. One may argue that even talking about the natural rate is not appropriate, because there is no one rate in the economy. Instead, the economy consists of different loans to different borrowers, each with unique risks and therefore different rates. However, for convenience, in this book we will talk about the natural rate. Many other commentators discuss total inflation and aggregate prices, while of course prices of different goods and services move differently. Therefore, it is probably also ok to talk about overall natural interest rates.

The natural rate of interest is somewhat of a similar concept to the risk free rate of interest. This is the rate of return that carries zero risk, or more specifically, zero counterparty risk. This can be obtained by lending money directly to the government, purchasing government bonds. In theory, the risk of the government defaulting is zero in countries where the government can both print its own currency and has a legal obligation to repay the debt. Therefore, all other interest rates in the currency should be above this floor interest rate, as other interest rates have some risks, which require compensation. This risk free rate therefore often drives all other rates in the economy.

There has never been widespread agreement on what the ideal natural rate of interest is for any given period or economy, or how to calculate it. Nor is there widespread agreement as to whether authorities should seek to set or cap interest rates or leave it up to the market to determine rates. Part of the difficulty is that there is no universal agreement on what natural interest rates fundamentally are or which factors and dynamics they should be linked to. Below we briefly discuss four alternative views.

1. **Returns on assets and growth** - As was mentioned in chapter one, this growth framework was probably how interest rates were originally determined. Loans can be provided to invest in assets which produce goods and services or yield a return. It therefore seems only fair that a lender should receive a share of this growth. The natural rate of interest can therefore be contrasted to the overall growth rate in the economy: GDP growth. The natural rate should be less than the GDP growth rate, but not too far behind it, or it may cause overinvestment, asset price bubbles and then inflation. Of course, some people borrow money for consumption, rather than investment. For consumption driven loans, this growth framework may not be appropriate.

2. **Time preference** - Another framework by which to evaluate interest rates is time. Interest rates can be thought of as the price of time. People are thought to prefer instant gratification rather than delays. Interest rates represent the price of locking up capital, such that one can enjoy the benefits of their labour at some point later on in time. The natural rate of interest therefore represents society's collective impatience. This theory seems more applicable to loans related to consumption, although it can also apply to investment related loans.

3. **Supply and demand for credit** - Interest rates can also be thought of as not only the price of time, but the price of

money. In an economy there is a level of demand for credit and a level of supply (savings). The interest rate is the equilibrium rate at which the market clears and supply and demand are in balance. The equilibrium rate will therefore encourage the correct amount of saving and investment. Interpreting the natural rate in this framework depends on the nature of money. In a gold system, a new discovery of gold can increase the money supply and therefore reduce the natural interest rate. In a debt based monetary system, the system we have today, where banks create money by issuing loans, this framework may be somewhat circular in reasoning as a tool to determine the natural rate. In the current climate, the willingness and ability of banks to lend may not be entirely dependent on market forces, but instead banking regulations such as reserve requirements, capital ratios and central bank liquidity provisioning. Therefore, this framework may not be appropriate.

4. **Monetary phenomenon** - The natural interest rate could also be a purely monetary phenomenon, driven by central bank policies and commercial banks expanding credit. One can argue that this means the natural interest rate is manipulated and not really linked to the real world. Today, central banks typically target a 2% inflation rate and officially alter the base interest rate to achieve this objective. There was also often an objective to keep unemployment low. Therefore, interest rates can be determined indirectly by consumer price levels. However, according to Goodhart's law: "Any observed statistical regularity will tend to collapse once pressure is placed upon it for control purposes".[25] In other words, when inflation becomes a target, it becomes a poor measure for the natural interest rate. Therefore, again, using the interest rate as a control stick to determine inflation may be somewhat circular in logic. Therefore, when interest rates are used as a monetary

---

[25] Problems of Monetary Management: UK Experience

> tool, we may not achieve a reasonable natural or equilibrium rate.

One can therefore argue that the natural interest rate can be determined by some complex combination of the above competing theories. However, this is probably quite difficult given the complexities involved here. The natural interest rate is often determined by an unclear and weak methodology and interpreting the rate and trying to assign meaning to it can be quite challenging. However, the fourth system listed above, the monetary phenomenon, however flawed, arbitrary and circular its logic is, seems to be the main driver of the natural interest rate in the modern economy.

When looking for correlations, history doesn't strongly support any of the above factors as the main driver of interest rates. Instead, typically natural interest rates appear to be driven by the peculiarities of the time, circumstance, or they are just manipulated. Interest rates seem mostly path-dependent, rather than being linked to any particular characteristics of the real world or economies. And while this looks to be the case through history, the same also appears true today.

Value Of Time

Perhaps the most philosophically perplexing paradigm in which to evaluate interest rates is time. Time preference is the idea that people prefer instant gratification, rather than delayed gratification. The interest rate can therefore be thought of as the price of time, the price for delaying gratification.

There is a rational argument for supporting the thesis that humans prefer instant gratification. Afterall life is inherently uncertain, anyone could die tomorrow. Therefore, bringing forward consumption reduces risk and uncertainty. There is also the logic of necessity. Perhaps some people have no choice but to bring forward consumption immediately, in order to survive. Only if they have accumulated sufficient savings can they afford the luxury of delayed gratification.

The 1972 Stanford marshmallow experiment, conducted by psychologist Walter Mischel, is often considered a key study in delayed gratification.[26] Nursery school aged children were offered one marshmallow immediately, or two after a delay of 15 minutes. An annualised interest rate of over 3.5 million percent. More recently, the experiment has become a meme online, with parents performing the test on their kids, filming the result and posting it on social media.[27] The experiment showed that a majority of children ate the marshmallow before the 15 minutes was up. Whilst perhaps the experiment was more about temptation than interest rates, it does illustrate that there is a cost of delayed gratification, perhaps more than just the uncertainty.

The extent to which delayed gratification is really less desirable than instant gratification now can be considered somewhat of a philosophical question or even a paradox. One cannot always delay consumption indefinitely, if one is always accumulating wealth and never spending, one will never enjoy the fruits of their labour. This was humorously explored in Lewis Carroll's 1871 book "Through the Looking-Glass":

> *"It's very good jam," said the Queen.*
> *"Well, I don't want any today, at any rate."*
> *"You couldn't have it if you did want it," the Queen said.*
> *"The rule is, jam tomorrow and jam yesterday – but never jam today."*
> *"It must come sometimes to 'jam today'," Alice objected.*
> *"No, it can't," said the Queen. "It's jam every other day: today isn't any other day, you know."[28]*

---

[26] https://psycnet.apa.org/record/1971-02138-001
[27] https://www.youtube.com/watch?v=QX_oy9614HQ
[28] Through the Looking-Glass

With regards to the natural interest rate, if it is society's collective price of impatience, we can make some assumptions. Perhaps an older, wealthier, healthier, more educated, harmonious society will experience lower interest rates. The improvement in technology and structure of society could therefore explain why interest rates have been declining for hundreds of years. Perhaps this could also explain why interest rates are especially low in Japan and partly explain the recent low rates in the West, but perhaps not the extremes seen post 2009. The zero or even negative rates we have witnessed recently cannot be explained within this time framework. The price of time explanation is hopeless at explaining negative rates. Only some kind of time machine or property of relativistic time dilation perhaps, could explain negative interest rates.

The Wrong Rate

If usury is the sin of interest rates being too high and exploitative, then one may ask what are the problems associated with interest rates being kept arbitrarily too low called? There does not seem to be a name for this, but the disadvantages of interest rates which are too low are very real. Some of these potential problems are outlined below:

- **Overconsumption** - The most obvious problem with the natural rate being too low is too much consumer consumption, driven by unsustainable borrowing. People could borrow too much money, which they cannot afford to pay back, attracted by an arbitrarily low natural rate of interest and causing them to become too indebted. People could consume more resources than the economy can support and this arbitrary overconsumption could also damage the environment through pollution to a greater extent than if consumption were at more natural levels.

- **Overinvestment** - Arbitrarily low interest rates could also cause too much investment, in particular investment in long term projects could be too high at the expense of projects with shorter time horizons. Much of this investment could be malinvestment if there are not enough real resources in the economy necessary to support the investments. Some projects which should never have been started could therefore fail to complete. With funding so cheap, companies could invest in projects that make very little sense, with time horizons that exceed the duration of the management team's expected term in office.

- **Funds trapped in the financial system** - Another major criticism of arbitrarily low interest rates, is that the cheap funding remains trapped in the financial system and does not enter the real economy. For example, banks are often accused of hoarding the cheap cash and not loaning it out to real businesses. Banks also tend to be accused of only making loans to hedge funds and financial speculators, rather than to real businesses connected to ordinary people. Financiers and speculators therefore tend to benefit from the low interest rates, while the real economy continues to suffer as there may be no effective transmission mechanism to link the low interest rates to the real economy.

- **Inequality** - Interest rates which are too low can also contribute to inequality in society. Typically, only large financial institutions and the rich have access to low interest rates, while in a kind of interest rate apartheid, the poor do not. Interest rates which are too low can push up asset prices, such as property, which tend to be held by the wealthy. This can then contribute to an economic divide, with those that are not on the property ladder or who don't own financial assets being left behind, with no hope of catching up.

- **Flow of funds overseas or to unscrupulous areas to obtain yield** - With the natural interest rate too low, investors hunting for yield may deploy capital overseas, where rates may be higher. This may weaken the value of the local currency and force investors, repressed by low returns, to invest in unscrupulous projects or schemes which promise higher returns, such as scams.

- **Asset price bubbles** - Artificially low interest rates can push up the price of land and financial assets. This positive price momentum, coupled with a continuing flow of cheaper and cheaper money, can cause frenetic fear of missing out (FOMO) driven price bubbles and speculation. This can then lead to bust and recession.

- **Does not help the economy anyway** - If interest rates are held at exceptionally low levels, some argue that the supposed benefits of low interest rates no longer apply and that the real economy does not benefit at all. For example, if interest rates are below 0%, it may have reached a kind of behavioural limit. At 0% ordinary people can detect that something is severely wrong with the economy and as rates get lower, rather than boosting consumption, lower rates can actually cause less spending. Very low interest rates can also cause bank profitability to decline, due to lower net interest margins, which could result in banks being less eager to lend.

- **Consumer price inflation** - Eventually, the impact of the low interest rates and higher money supply could enter the real economy, resulting in higher consumer prices. This may then result in people being unable to afford core necessities such as food, shelter and energy. It can result in a cost-of-living crisis.

The Inflation Targeting Orthodoxy

From the 1990s onwards, the orthodoxy from the authorities and central banks was all about inflation targeting. This applied across the developed world, in Japan, Europe and the United States. This inflation targeting framework was used to set target interest rates, while other considerations were mostly set aside. With such a focus on inflation, Goodhart's law became more and more applicable. Inflation became an unsuitable measure by which to set interest rates. Not only was price inflation the main focus, but there was an obsession with a particular inflation number, 2%, which became a global standard. It was as if 2% is a magic number of some sort, with almost all central banks around the world agreeing on it.

Since 1996, the Federal Reserve unofficially had a 2% inflation target, which finally became an official target under Ben Bernanke in January 2012.[29] The Bank of Japan formally set its price stability target at 2% in January 2013.[30] The European Central Bank has a 2% target in its constitution and the Bank of England also has a 2% inflation target, which it was given in 1997.

2008 Financial Crisis

In 1998, after the failure of Long Term Capital Management, a leveraged hedge fund, in order to calm financial markets, the Federal Reserve responded by cutting interest rates by 25 bps to 4.75%. The chairman of the Federal Reserve at the time was Alan Greenspan and the phrase "Greenspan Put" became popular. This was a play on the word "put option", the idea being that if conditions became tough, the Federal Reserve would ease, providing investors downside protection. These conditions were said to ensure stock prices kept on increasing in price.

At the end of the 1990s, a monumental bubble in technology and internet stocks occurred. The NASDAQ 100 composite increased in value by 414% from the end of 1997 to its peak in early 2000. The bubble was characterised by new internet companies that failed, such as pets.com, boo.com, and WorldCom, as well as companies that survived such as Amazon.com and Cisco Systems.

In early 2000 the technology bubble burst. The NASDAQ fell by around 85% from the peak to a low reached in October 2002. In response, the Federal Reserve cut interest rates. In 2000 the Federal funds rate was 6% and by late 2003 this fell to just 1%, this was an unprecedented rate, exceptionally low. This interest rate was far

---

[29] https://fredblog.stlouisfed.org/2020/11/from-inflation-targeting-to-average-inflation-targeting/
[30] https://www.boj.or.jp/en/mopo/outline/qqe.htm/

lower than the GDP growth rate in the US, which was around 4% in 2003. By 2004 the US economy picked up and was growing by over 6% per annum, yet interest rates remained well below this level. While growth was strong, inflation remained moderate and under control. By 2006 Ben Bernanke took over as chairman of the Federal Reserve. This period of moderate growth and low inflation was known as the "great moderation". British Chancellor Gordon Brown famously repeated the "end to boom and bust" slogan repeatedly in the 2004 to 2006 period[31], taking credit for the stable economic environment.

Following on from this period of stability, was the 2008 global financial crisis. A credit crisis where the solvency of banks and financial institutions was in question and contagion spread throughout the financial system. The epicentre of the crisis was the failure of Lehman Brothers in October 2008. A huge amount of material has been written on the financial crisis, with commentators and analysts blaming it on the following:

- Poor and insufficient banking regulations.
- Conflicts of interest and bad practices at credit rating agencies.
- Greed in the financial industry and too much unethical behaviour.
- The failure to separate investment banking from retail bank deposits (Glass-Steagall Act).
- The existence of credit default swaps and collateralised debt obligations.
- Too much government support in the subprime mortgage market.
- Inappropriate accounting standards.
- Inappropriate value at risk models, too focused on statistical theory rather than the real world.

---

[31] https://www.channel4.com/news/articles/politics/domestic_politics/factcheck%2Bno%2Bmore%2Bboom%2Band%2Bbust/2564157.html

Other commentators often described the crisis as a random event, a bit like an extreme hurricane or earthquake. A catastrophe with no particular cause that cannot be predicted, which just happens every now and again. While there is truth to some of the above reasons, in that they did contribute to the crisis and they were certainly catalysts, another theory is that interest rates were kept too low for too long beforehand. This may have suppressed volatility in financial markets, encouraging complacency and allowed too much leverage to build up. It is the policy response to the 2000 technology bubble bursting, which may have sowed the seeds for the next bubble, the housing bubble, which then burst in 2008. The 2008 global financial crisis can fundamentally be thought of as a story of interest rates being kept recklessly low. However, there is no consensus on this view. This interest rate theory was not the conventional view among the establishment at all. The Federal Reserve denied that its policies contributed to the 2008 financial crisis and other factors were blamed.

The Policy Response

In response to the 2008 crisis the Federal Reserve and other central banks launched an unprecedented stimulus. Interest rates were lowered again, this time to historically low levels. The Federal Reserve lowered the base interest rate to 0% at the end of 2008 and kept rates at this level for seven years. Rates then climbed a bit for a few years from 2016 to 2019, before going straight back to zero as the COVID-19 pandemic hit.

In addition to lowering interest rates, central banks and the authorities also engaged in other expansionary policies to deal with the aftermath of the crash and achieve their 2% inflation targets. This included the nationalisation of several financial institutions impacted by the crisis, emergency loan and liquidity swap schemes and plans to purchase or guarantee "toxic" assets from the distressed financial institutions to repair their balance sheets, such as TARP (Troubled Asset Relief Program) or TALF (Term Asset-Backed Securities Loan Facility). In addition to these schemes, the other most notable policy was something called quantitative easing (QE). This is where central banks purchase government bonds (or other financial assets), in order to increase the banking reserves in the system. This policy expands the balance sheets of the central banks and as the policy continues, it tends to result in the central banks holding a large proportion of their respective countries' national debt. This policy was enacted quite aggressively in Europe, the UK, Japan and the United States.

In a desperate effort to achieve the 2% inflation targets, some central banks even took interest rates negative. Sweden became the first bank to officially introduce negative interest rates in August 2009. The Swedish central bank set an interest rate of minus 0.25% for commercial banks who had deposits at the central bank.[32] The idea was that commercial banks were hoarding too much capital, keeping it as cash deposits and not making enough loans into the real economy. Negative interest rates would deter this hoarding and force banks to loan money into the economy. Evidence justifying this policy was provided, which included data about the significant increase of commercial bank deposits at the central bank (bank reserves), which showed they were not lending enough. Anyone with a strong understanding of money and banking knows this logic is fundamentally flawed.

The level of aggregate commercial bank deposits at the central bank is determined by central bank policy, not the willingness of commercial banks to make new loans. Only the central bank (by their policy actions) can create or destroy bank reserves. Quantitative easing created new bank reserves. Once these reserves are created they are trapped. Commercial banks can shuffle these reserves around between them, but they cannot remove them. Only when central banks taper, do these reserves decline. When large dominant commercial banks make new loans, this does not reduce their central bank reserves. New loans create new deposits in the banking system. This can be a challenging concept to grasp and it's important to think through the practicalities. If a commercial bank provides a mortgage,

---

[32] https://www.ft.com/content/5d3f0692-9334-11de-b146-00144feabdc0

the seller of the property does not redeem the funds at the central bank, depleting bank reserves. Instead, the seller typically keeps the funds on deposit in the banking system and therefore deposits increase.

Therefore, the main justification behind negative interest rates appears somewhat flawed. However, there is the idea that if banks make a loss on their reserves, they then need to take more risk with the other assets in order to generate a profit. There is some justification here, however this logic is somewhat weak and the negative interest rates certainly don't deter banks, as a group, from hoarding.

Despite the flimsy logic, negative interest rates continued. The central banks in Denmark and Switzerland also implemented negative rates and the European Central Bank itself also started charging negative interest rates on "excess" reserves. The negative interest rate in Europe lasted eight years, from June 2014 to July 2022.[33] In 2016 the Bank of Japan lowered its key rate to minus 0.1%. Negative interest rates were never officially adopted in the United States, although it was discussed as a potential idea.

Some banks in Europe and Japan passed on these negative rates to depositors. In Denmark, in 2019, banks offered the world's first negative interest mortgages. Jyske Bank is said to have offered customers a ten year deal at minus 0.5%.[34] At the peak of negative rates, in around 2020, there were over 4,500 bonds trading with a negative yield, with a market value of over US$18 trillion.[35] In March 2020, the German ten year government bond traded on a yield as low as minus 0.91%. In December 2020 a 100-year zero coupon Austrian government bond, traded on a yield of minus 0.01%. This means you could spend over 100 Euros today, for nothing except the right to potentially receive 100 Euros in the year 2120. That is assuming the

---

[33] https://www.ecb.europa.eu/stats/policy_and_exchange_rates/key_ecb_interest_rates/html/index.en.html
[34] https://www.theguardian.com/money/2019/aug/13/danish-bank-launches-worlds-first-negative-interest-rate-mortgage
[35] https://www.bloomberg.com/news/articles/2022-05-04/there-are-only-100-negative-yielding-bonds-left-in-the-world

Austrian government has not defaulted by then and if somehow you are still alive.

Quantitative easing also changed the mechanism by which central banks set interest rates. Prior to the financial crisis, central banks conducted open market operations which changed the level of bank reserves. Since these reserves were scarce, this was enough to influence short term interest rates. After quantitative easing started, this necessarily created excess reserves (that was the point of it), therefore open market operations were no longer sufficient to influence short term interest rates. After the financial crisis, the interest rates the central banks paid on excess reserves became an important tool. Therefore, some argued, changing the rate of interest on excess reserves, including charging negative rates, was a necessary tool to ensure natural interest rates reached the desired level.

In 2020, as the response to the COVID-19 pandemic hit the global economy, the authorities responded with even more stimulus. In March 2020, in the United States, interest rates went back down to zero again and the Trump administration passed a US$2.2 trillion stimulus bill. The bill included US$300 billion of cash payments to all Americans who pay taxes. That is around US$1,200 per person. In addition to this, hundreds of billions of "forgivable loans" to businesses were provided. The Biden administration passed a similar US$1.9 trillion package in March 2021. In total many people received three rounds of direct cash payments: US$1,200 in April 2020, US$600 in December 2020 and US$1,400 in March 2021. There were similar unprecedented programs in other countries, except they typically involved directly making a monthly payment to those who could not work due to COVID-19. Paying people to do nothing rather than produce. The era of helicopter money had finally truly arrived.

5

Everything Bubble

After the 2008 financial crisis, perhaps as a result of the monetary policy enacted in response to it, the prices of a whole range of assets soared. This is sometimes referred to as the everything bubble. In 2000 it was technology stocks, in 2008 it was primarily housing and by this third wave of lower interest rates, it was pretty much absolutely every asset with a price.

The first major bubble post the global financial crisis was in commodities. Some rare earth metals rallied up to 4,000% between January 2010 and the peak at the end of May 2011. These metals such as cerium, praseodymium and europium were said to be powering new technology such as iPhones and would be hoarded by the Chinese government as a key strategic asset. Gold rallied 181% from its post-financial crisis low to US$1,921 a troy ounce by its 2011 high, as the unprecedented easing undermined the integrity of fiat money. In the eyes of some investors gold was still seen as an alternative to fiat paper money. Silver also enjoyed a massive run, up 489% from its post-financial crisis low to almost US$50 a troy ounce by May 2011. Agricultural commodities saw a boom too, corn increased in value by 191% from its post-financial crisis low to its peak in 2012. Oil also enjoyed a similar boom in the period, rallying 185%.

These commodity bubbles fizzled out and prices crashed between mid-2011 to 2012. Improving technology in mining and large capital investments in production capacity pre the global financial crisis, ensured production growth and therefore the supply of the commodities was strong. At the same time, commodities, traditionally a good area for bubbles, didn't really capture the imagination of millennials or the zeitgeist of the time. In contrast, the areas highlighted and discussed below, enjoyed a sensational bubble that in some form or another, persisted up until 2021. In some cases, these bubbles lasted over 10 years.

Everything Bubble Indicators & Examples

Loss making IPOs - By 2018 the percentage of IPOs consisting of unprofitable companies listing on public markets reached a record high of over 80%.[36] Re-taking the previous high in the 1999 technology bubble. This compares to a low of around 30% in 2009. With interest rates near zero, short term profitability mattered less and less to investors, who were instead focused on the long-term growth prospects.

FAANGs - FAANG stands for Facebook, Apple, Amazon, Netflix and Google. Examples of exceptionally strong and dominant technology companies, with good growth prospects. Due to the almost monopoly position of each of these companies, they were said to be unstoppable and would continue to grow into perpetuity. Conventional wisdom was that it did not matter what price you invested in these stocks, as the growth would eventually catch up with you. Apple, the most valuable company of the five, became the world's first trillion dollar company in August 2018. Then two years later it achieved a two trillion dollar valuation, before finally, in January 2022, breaching the three trillion dollar mark.

Buybacks - With money so cheap, it made sense for corporations to borrow. One thing they did with the money is buy back their own stock. In 2021 S&P 500 companies purchased a record US$881.7 billion of their own stock, a 69.6% increase from the $519.8 billion in 2020.[37] Some companies, such as Intel and IBM, were accused of

---
[36] https://www.ruffer.co.uk/en/thinking/articles/the-green-line/2019-06-the-green-line
[37] https://www.prnewswire.com/news-releases/sp-500-buybacks-set-quarterly-and-annual-record-301502561.html

spending too much money on buybacks, rather than investing in technology, resulting in a weaker strategic position.

Corporate Debt - In 2020 US non-financial corporate debt reached US$27.7 trillion, a record high and up 9.2% compared to 2020. This compares to total US corporate debt of around US$10 trillion before the 2008 global financial crisis.[38]

Real Estate - Real estate markets around the world also reacted positively to financial conditions. The boom was global, with cities such as New York, London, Sydney, Vancouver and Hong Kong seeing strong price appreciation in the value of property, in particular the prime sectors. The London house price index increased by 114% between the 2009 low and 2022.[39]

Art - Art prices also reached record highs. At the time of writing, every one of the fifteen most expensive paintings ever sold, in official inflation adjusted dollars, occurred after the 2008 financial crisis. Auction house Sotheby's generated US$7.3 billion of revenues in 2021, a record high, up 46% YoY.

Startups - The post crisis period was one of extraordinary success for startups and venture capital investors. Venture capital funds such as Andreessen Horowitz, Sequoia Capital, Kleiner Perkins, Accel, Index Ventures, Lightspeed Ventures, Greylock Partners were the new masters of the universe, replacing investment banks from the pre-crisis era. They were the new Goldman Sachs, where all the graduates wanted to go to make money. The VC firms tend to operate as a pack, all competing with each other over deal flow, keen to be first into the next big thing. Raising money as a technology startup was never easier, if one had the right connections. One just needed the ability to sell a dream. The firms never even needed to make profits in order for the VC funds to capitalise on it, they could just keep raising more VC money in more rounds at higher valuation

---

[38] https://www.statista.com/statistics/1075320/total-nonfinancial-corporation-debt-major-economies/
[39] Nationwide

points and then eventually conduct a loss-making IPO. In 2021, US$330 billion of VC money was invested in the United States, up 99% YoY and up almost 1,200% since 2009.[40] There is also significant "dry powder" remaining for new investments, American VC funds are said to currently be sitting on US$230 billion of capital.[41]

Concept stocks - The valuations of companies that capture the public imagination of the future, reached astronomical levels. Some examples of these concepts and ideas, along with the associated stocks, are listed below:

- Electric cars (Tesla, Nicola)
- Electric car batteries (CATL)
- Robotics (Teradyne)
- Home sharing (AirBnB)
- Food delivery (Deliveroo)
- Office space (WeWork)
- Ride sharing companies (Uber, Lyft)
- Cannabis legalisation (Curaleaf, Sundial Growers)
- E-cigarettes (Zandera, CN Creative)
- Fake meat (Beyond Meat)
- Home exercising (Peloton)
- Zero fee stock trading (Robinhood)
- Blockchains (Marathon Digital, Bakkt)

Meme stocks - The meme stock craze, where trading in a particular name becomes popular through social media, such as the subreddit /r/wallstreetbets, started in 2021. The meme stock phenomena is characterised by young traders, who are not financial professionals, investing in a stock or its call options, without any consideration for its valuation. The traders are often looking for stocks where large short positions exist, such that a short squeeze can occur and the stock rally can therefore be especially frenetic. This famously happened to

---
[40] https://www.statista.com/statistics/277501/venture-capital-amount-invested-in-the-united-states-since-1995/
[41] https://uk.finance.yahoo.com/news/venture-capital-is-seeing-a-slowdown-sidelines-133309996.html

Gamestop. Other names impacted by this are the cinema chain AMC and Bed, Bath & Beyond. From the start of 2021 to its peak less than a month later, Gamestop appreciated in price by over 2,330%.

Cryptocurrency - At perhaps the epicentre of the bubble was the world of cryptocurrency. Bitcoin itself had a series of four fantastic rallies in 2011, 2013, 2017 and 2021. However, this is only the tip of the iceberg with respect to the insanity and outrageous valuations in the cryptocurrency space. From "The DAO" (Decentralised Autonomous Organisation) in 2016, to the 2017 ICO boom, the 2017 chain splits which generated value out of nothing, the 2021 DeFi governance token boom, the 2021 food token boom, the re-emergence of DAOs in 2021 and the dog coin bubble. Then there is the high yield cryptocurrency stablecoin and lending markets, designed to capitalise on these booms, which is a topic extensively covered later in this book.

NFTs - In 2021 there was a massive boom in the prices and trading volume of non-fungible tokens. These tokens which exist on blockchains, such as Ethereum, are typically associated with an image file. In March 2021 an artist known as Beeple famously sold an NFT for $69m.[42] Part of the reason for the purchase was that the buyer was a fund which already had a large number of NFTs and this large purchase could generate media hype that could boost the value of the portfolio. In August 2021 a twelve year old British schoolboy is said to have made £290,000 from creating the Weird Whale NFTs.[43] The most expensive NFT in the Ether Rock series went for US$1.8 million[44], quite a lot for a digital token somehow linked to a basic Microsoft Paint style drawing of a plain grey rock. Then of course there is the Bored Ape Yacht Club (BAYC). This collection of 10,000 NFTs are images of apes each with slightly different features, the project launched in April 2021. The company behind this was Yuga Labs, which in March 2022 launched an APE token that traded at a peak market capitalisation of over US$6 billion. The apes

---
[42] https://www.theverge.com/2021/3/11/22325054/beeple-christies-nft-sale-cost-everydays-69-million
[43] https://www.bbc.co.uk/news/technology-58343062
[44] https://twitter.com/etherrockprice/status/1455419941834956800

themselves trade at exorbitant prices, with the most expensive sale being ape number 8,817, which sold for US$3.4 million in October 2021.[45] The ape depicted has solid gold fur, which is said to be a rare trait, improving its value in the eyes of some investors, along with its silver ear ring. These apes are culturally significant, with celebrity owners said to include Justin Bieber, Madonna, Neymar, Paris Hilton and Jimmy Fallon. Whether these celebrities actually had to pay for the apes, or whether an NFT broker or facilitator provided it to them, in order to boost the value of the apes, is not always clear. For example, some of the celebrities mentioned above are said to be shareholders in NFT broker and trading facilitator MoonPay.[46]

Metaverse real estate - 2021 saw a boom in the value of square land plots in virtual worlds such as Sandbox and Decentraland, known as Metaverses. Towards the end of 2021 the average price of a plot of land in Decentraland was over US$40,000.[47] In November 2021 one plot was sold for as much as $2.4 million.[48] Investment groups such as Metaverse Group spent millions of dollars on these plots. Metaverse Group had a portfolio of assets which included 227 Decentraland plots, 65 Sandbox plots and 11 Somium plots as of August 2022. Despite attracting significant investor flow in 2021, these virtual worlds were typically dull and empty, with a very limited number of people actually using or engaging with them. The dream of owning these plots was that they could earn a yield. Perhaps "land" owners could sell advertising space if the plot had high user traffic passing by. Alternatively, the owner could build a property on their land and then the plot could be rented out, perhaps to a corporation hosting a virtual event. With interest rates in the real economy at recklessly low levels, virtual brothels were even considered as a form of income[49] as virtual land changed hands for exorbitant prices.

---

[45] https://twitter.com/Sothebysverse/status/1453042450788982794
[46] https://fortune.com/2022/04/13/justin-bieber-gwyneth-paltrow-diplo-drake-investors-crypto-payments-startup-moonpay-nfts/
[47] https://cointelegraph.com/news/metaverse-housing-bubble-bursting-virtual-land-prices-crash-85-amid-waning-interest
[48] https://content.techgig.com/technology/virtual-land-sold-for-record-2-4-million-in-metaverse/articleshow/87888005.cms
[49] https://exoduscry.com/articles/kids-are-welcomed-into-metaverse-brothels-and-strip-clubs/

In addition to the above, there are more examples of the everything bubble. The bubble was by no means spread evenly across the economy. In general, it is the wealthy that enjoyed the most benefits. Areas that grew significant post the 2008 financial crisis include: Private jets, wine, super cars, yachts, luxury handbags, luxury watches and diamonds, to name a few. Meanwhile, a majority of people, who don't own financial assets, were somewhat left behind during the boom.

Are Interest Rates Important Anymore?

Some economists argue that the low interest rates are not especially important to the real economy anymore. Not that many people have variable rate mortgages and are therefore not particularly impacted by the lower interest rates they cannot access anyway. However, this may be entirely the point. As interest rates reached record lows and went negative, it is not ordinary people in the real economy that benefited. It is the asset owners and the fake bubble economy, which was impacted considerably, while the so-called real economy disintegrated to some extent. Artificially low interest rates appear to have taken the economic fuel away from real, hardworking, sustainable, profitable and humble people and companies. Instead, we had a fake bubble economy, with narcissistic leaders, characterised by extravagance and madness.

The flip side of this is that some of these highly financialised sectors of the economy and any businesses depending on them could be hit hard by tightening financial conditions and higher interest rates. These areas are extremely sensitive to financial flows and liquidity conditions. Any tightening in policy, an increase in rates, may have a significant impact here.

2022 Inflation

Halfway through 2021, the official inflation rate (CPI) in the US started to increase above the 2% target, reaching 5.2%. By mid-2022, the annual inflation rate continued to climb and reached 8.5%. The high inflation and the cost-of-living crisis became perhaps the most significant political issue. Finally, the official data showed that the costs of goods and services which ordinary people need: food and energy, were starting to rapidly appreciate. Ordinary people were starting to feel the pain.

In general (there are some notable exceptions), the high inflation took the political and economic establishment by complete surprise. It could be said they were complacent and did not appropriately assess the inflationary risks. In January 2022, American president Joe Biden was asked by a reporter: "Do you think inflation is a political liability ahead of the midterms?" The president replied by saying:

> *No, it's a great asset. More inflation. What a stupid son of a bitch.* [50]

The implication being that Joe Biden still thought low inflation was a more significant risk than high inflation, which was of course the establishment and consensus view over the last 30 years. The president and most policymakers appeared slow to come to terms with the new reality. Throughout 2021 and early 2022, as inflation picked up, the buzzword among treasury officials and central bankers was that the inflation was only "transitory".[51]

The debate on the cause of inflation was also starting to intensify. One of the main narratives put forward in this book is that the low interest rates and loose monetary policy caused an "everything bubble". The bubble was initially focused on financial assets and other luxury items only consumed by the ultra-wealthy, before eventually leaking out into the real economy. Just as Richard Cantillon had astutely observed almost exactly 300 years earlier, the liquidity was initially trapped in the financial system, before

---

[50] https://www.whitehouse.gov/briefing-room/speeches-remarks/2022/01/24/remarks-by-president-biden-before-meeting-with-the-white-house-competition-council/
[51] https://www.cnbc.com/2022/06/01/yellen-says-the-administration-is-fighting-inflation-admits-she-was-wrong-that-it-was-transitory.html

eventually being released into the real economy. One group had benefited from the new money first, the well-connected elites, before the cost of the new money impacted the rest of society.

There is no universal consensus that the loose monetary policy caused the inflation. Just as occurred with the 2008 global financial crisis, a whole range of potential causes were identified. Left wing American congresswomen Alexandria Ocasio-Cortez said in July 2021:

> *If this was an overall inflationary issue, we would see prices going up in relatively equal amounts, across the board no matter what the good is. But we know what is getting expensive, things like the cost of lumber, items like cars, whether they are new or used and other sorts of items that rely on shipping or shipping containers coming from overseas. These are very sector specific which means that they are due to supply chain issues, that means we don't have enough ports that can accommodate all of the backed up ships that are trying to come in. It is because we don't have enough computer chips, that are produced by a handful of factories in the world.*[52]

Typically, those on the left and centre of politics did not attribute the loose monetary policy as the cause. Instead, they often blamed peculiarities in individual industries and supply chain distribution problems due to the lockdowns caused by COVID-19. These volatile and unpredictable supply chain disruptions then rippled through the economy, making it harder to manage inventory levels, resulting in higher prices in some periods.

In February 2022, the Russian president Vladmir Putin decided to engage in an invasion of Ukraine. This resulted in a wave of sanctions against Russia and a spike in oil and gas prices. Gas became a main strategic focus of the war, with gas supplies to Europe from Russia

---

[52] https://twitter.com/repaoc/status/1417515082863554561

being cut off. This war gave many political commentators and economic analysts something new to blame for the inflation. It was Vladmir Putin's inflation.

These different and somewhat competing narratives over the cause of inflation are not necessarily inconsistent. Complex and dynamic systems like inflation can be looked at from multiple valid angles. There are always inflationary and deflationary pressures operating at the same time. Perhaps both the economic shutdown because of COVID-19, Putin and the 15 years of ultra-loose monetary policy all contributed to inflation and the combined impact of all of these factors overcame the deflationary forces. Alternatively, perhaps the COVID-19 supply chain shutdowns acted as a catalyst, to initiate inflation, in an economy already susceptible to inflationary pressure due to the loose monetary policy.

It is important to appreciate that the economy is a dynamic path-dependent and complex system. Once consumer price inflation gains traction, it can be challenging to assess how it will change over time and difficult to smoothly bring it back under control. When one considers the possibility of feedback loops involving the beliefs of a technology-savvy, social media driven, paranoid and fanatical public, inflation is not likely to emerge as a linear or mechanical type of phenomenon, which can easily be controlled. Instead, inflation may operate more like an unpredictable beast, rampaging across all areas of the economy. Once this is set in motion, inflation expectations could be volatile for many years. The authorities may find that it's easier to burst the asset bubble than tame consumer price inflation in the real economy. Facing this challenge, it is possible there is a prolonged period of more volatile and weaker returns for holders of financial assets.

Rising Rates

As a result of rising inflation, reluctantly the Federal Reserve had to act. Between March 2022 to September 2022, the base interest rates in the United States increased from near 0% to 3.25%. Europe has taken the same course. As many financial speculators and investors have grown used to these low rates, the shock is likely to impact financial assets. The everything bubble could burst, the FAANGs, concept stocks, meme stocks, cryptocurrency and NFTs are likely to be hit. This process is already under way. If financial markets are impacted, after a lag, the impact of this may then trickle down into the real economy and inflation may come down. However, inflation may not then remain calm for a prolonged period. Volatile financial asset prices may lead to a volatile and changing policy response, with policy makers always chasing their tails. Inflation is unlikely to be tame for long.

At the same time, as central banks tighten, the mechanics of unwinding their expansionary policies may not be as smooth as on the way up. Quantitative easing created excess reserves which were trapped in the financial system for years. On the way down we may witness how banks became used to these reserves and how they now play a different and important role in supporting banking operations and liquidity. Banks now depend on these reserves. If this unwinds too fast, it may restrict the willingness and capability of the banks to lend into the economy.

The Federal Reserve's reverse repurchase agreement operations (repo market), which is when the Federal Reserve sells an asset to an eligible financial counterparty with an agreement to buy it back in the future, has grown considerably in the last few years. The Federal Reserve buys these assets back, at a price equivalent to the interest rate. As the Federal Reserve is selling the asset for "cash", this transaction reduces bank reserves. On Tuesday 17 September 2019, the reverse repo market interest rate, which is normally always stable, experienced a sudden spike to 10%. The cause of this spike may have been a shortage of reserves in the banking system, despite the elevated levels of reserves caused by quantitative easing. The Federal Reserve then had to take emergency action, stepping in and supplying US$75 billion in liquidity to push these rates back down.

As policy rates have risen, this reverse repo tool is more attractive to financial counterparties. At the time of writing, the pool of assets under this agreement is US$2.4 trillion.[53] It is possible this reverse repo balance continues to expand as interest rates rise and that this could be the pressure point that drains banks of the reserves they now need. This crisis could then force the Federal Reserve to reverse course and provide banks more cash reserves. Firstly with an emergency scheme and then perhaps with lower rates. Round and round in circles we go. With the circles getting smaller and smaller.

There are still plenty of defenders of central bank policy around. They would contend that interest rates and other expansionary measures are not the primary driver of economic conditions. Post 2008, we had a natural deflationary environment. The accommodative policy was merely offsetting this. The policies may have contributed to higher asset prices and inequality; however this was necessary to offset the prevailing deflationary conditions. In 2022, conditions started to change and inflationary pressures started to pick up due to factors unrelated to central bank policy. Central banks then responded appropriately, by dampening the inflation with higher rates.

One can make up their own mind as to whether monetary policy has become so extreme that it is the most significant driver of economic conditions or whether humble central bankers are carefully dampening conditions in a very difficult and challenging climate. At least in the Bitcoin world, at least in the pre-2017 Bitcoin world anyway, opinion is not especially divided. It is the former option, rather than the latter, which is considered correct.

---

[53] https://fred.stlouisfed.org/series/RRPONTSYD

6

Bitcoin Interest Rate

The Invention Of Bitcoin

On 31st October 2008, in the middle of the most intense period of the financial implosion of the 2008 global financial crisis, a whitepaper was published by a pseudonymous individual called Satoshi Nakamoto. The groundbreaking paper described a new transformational type of money, Bitcoin. Bitcoin was the world's first decentralised electronic money. Bitcoin required no banks and no central banks, instead users could run the core financial infrastructure themselves, on their home computers and engage in peer-to-peer electronic unblockable bearer like transactions, without trusting financial intermediaries. The timing of the launch was absolutely perfect, right when trust in banks was at a historic low.

In the eyes of Bitcoin supporters, Bitcoin was a revolutionary new technology, set to free the world of the ills of the banking and economic system and provide much needed financial freedom to the masses. Bitcoin was an unstoppable positive force, which would act as a tool to resist authoritarian governments, disrupt the inefficient and corrupt financial architecture and provide services to the world's poor and unbanked. At the same time, Bitcoin supporters and investors would benefit financially, as others began to realise Bitcoin's incredible transformational potential.

On the other hand, sceptics viewed Bitcoin as a joke, another tulip mania. Paying money for a token that was totally virtual made no sense and it would surely collapse in price. At the same time, they viewed the typical Bitcoiner diagnosis of society's economic problems as flawed and naive.

As Bitcoin continued to grow and appreciate in price, the view of Bitcoin sceptics pivoted. It was no longer seen as a useless scam, guaranteed to end in catastrophic failure. Opponents of Bitcoin changed their minds, they started to see it also as a revolutionary new and transformational technology. Not as a way to solve problems with the financial plumbing in the economy, but instead as a new, fascinating and perfect object of speculation and price bubbles. Bubbles which persisted far longer than they expected. Through this lens, the timing of Bitcoin's launch was also perfect. Bitcoin launched at the same time as central banks engaged on a path of unprecedented easing and record low interest rates, fuelling financial speculative bubbles. This greatly benefited Bitcoin, causing it to appreciate in value at an incredible pace.

However, Bitcoin is not the *perfect* object of speculation. One can do better. Bitcoin has no inherent interest rate or yield. Bitcoin's critics often compare it to a ponzi scheme, however ponzi schemes typically have a yield or promised rate of return. For example, Charles Ponzi, whom this kind of scheme is named after, famously promised his clients a 50% profit in 45 days.[54] That is not to say there were no ponzi schemes and other scams inside the Bitcoin space. These scams and promises of extraordinary returns have indeed attracted large amounts of capital into the cryptocurrency ecosystem. However, the Bitcoin protocol itself promises no yield. If one merely buys Bitcoin, one either wants to use Bitcoin or one is hoping to benefit from price appreciation. Had Bitcoin been designed purely as an object of perfect speculation, it could have attempted to include a yield in the core protocol. Some alternative coins have adopted schemes like this. In September 2022, Ethereum switched to Proof of Stake and under this system, the phrase "perfect object of speculation" to describe Ethereum, may be even more appropriate.

---

[54] https://web.archive.org/web/20110623060130/http://www.time.com/time/magazine/article/0,9171,930255,00.html

Bitcoin does of course have Proof of Work mining, where newly issued coins are allocated to miners who extend the Bitcoin blockchain. This business activity does have potential returns and therefore a yield. However, Bitcoin mining is very much an industrial process, one needs to purchase and operate expensive unstable equipment and use large amounts of energy. Much of the value here leaks out of Bitcoin to equipment manufacturers and energy producers. Bitcoin mining is a risky industrial process, not a way to generate passive income. Proudhon's 1849 critique, that interest is a "reward for idleness" is not applicable here. While for Proof of Stake systems, the criticism may be more valid.

The Bitcoin Interest Rate

With no yield or interest rate built into the Bitcoin protocol, a Bitcoin interest rate will only emerge if people start to borrow and lend Bitcoin. Given the complexity and uncertainty of how to determine the interest rate, it is quite challenging to evaluate interest rates in the context of Bitcoin. What if people start to make loans in Bitcoin? What rates will they charge and how could we interpret these interest rates?

Bitcoin has a fixed and known issuance rate. There will only ever be 21 million coins and new coins are only issued on a fixed schedule known in advance. Therefore, Bitcoin interest rates cannot be a monetary phenomenon. At least the interest rate should not change due to monetary policy changes. However, the Bitcoin protocol only replaces central banks in this context. Commercial Bitcoin lenders could still lend out Bitcoin they do not have, expanding credit just like they do with fiat money. However, the level of credit expansion under a Bitcoin system is probably not likely to reach the scale it does with fiat money. The lending institution may feel it is always under a certain type of pressure, that depositors could always ask for their Bitcoin back and demand it on-chain. This kind of pressure does not exist in the fiat system, as funds are locked into the banking system unless they are redeemed in the form of physical cash. This form of redemption is not likely to happen at scale, as holding physical cash has various logistical problems. There is a risk for Bitcoin though, if the Bitcoin deposit taking institutions are vertically integrated with the providers of custody technology and the end clients don't have the capability to custody the funds themselves. If this happens Bitcoin will look more and more like a fiat money system. At least for now, this has not happened to the extent required to materially undermine Bitcoin's supply properties. For now, the Bitcoin interest rate will not be driven by monetary considerations. And therefore other factors will determine Bitcoin interest rates.

The supply cap, Bitcoin's economic critics proclaim, is a major weakness. As a result of it, in a Bitcoin based economy, there will be deflation and slow growth. This will reduce consumption, as people hoard money. The interest rate could also be too high, which will cause underinvestment, due to a lack of demand to borrow at high rates and therefore the economy will not grow at a decent rate. This could result in widespread poverty. Even if there are Bitcoin denominated investment and loans, in the event of an economic slowdown there is nothing the authorities could do to stimulate the economy by lowering rates. Debt Deflation would persist and be a major problem and the economy could stagnate for long periods of time. Companies and people could be stuck with large growing debt burdens and interest payments they could not afford. Of course, it's ironic that Bitcoin's economic critics make these points. Bitcoin is extremely unlikely to become a major investment currency and from the perspective of Bitcoin's critics, the chances of this should be laughingly tiny. Therefore, from their point of view it is unclear why these critics spend so much time articulating a potential problem; that will never actually materialise.

Part of the dream of Bitcoin, to many of its supporters, is a form of money free from manipulation. This means both that the authorities cannot censor transactions and also that the authorities cannot alter the supply or engage in manipulative monetary policies, which many Bitcoiners consider to have been destructive to the economy. In particular, the accusation is that interest rates have been kept too low for too long. Under a Bitcoin system, interest rates could be determined more freely, by the market. People can freely engage in lending arrangements without regulation and the invisible hand of the market will ensure that the return on assets, time preferences and supply and demand for credit of all market participants, consumers and investors, are all factored in. Since the Bitcoin supply is known, we no longer have the problem of a large gold discovery causing unexpected inflation. We also no longer have the problem of trying to calculate the natural rate of interest, whatever rate the market decides is the most appropriate rate. The prices of other goods and services in the economy are not set by the authorities, so why should the price of money be any different?

Throughout Bitcoin's history, Bitcoin borrowing has been considered inappropriate for various reasons. Firstly, the price has appreciated considerably. This raises the question as to why a borrower would even want a liability in Bitcoin, a liability that could keep increasing in value. There is no real significant circular Bitcoin economy emerging and no businesses have Bitcoin denominated revenues (perhaps with the exception of Bitcoin miners and Bitcoin financial services firms). Therefore, why would any business want a loan in an appreciating currency that doesn't match up with its revenue? Instead, most businesses would much prefer a fiat loan than a Bitcoin one. Only a small number of entities have borrowed in Bitcoin, normally for highly specialised purposes.

Whether an economic system with a free-floating Bitcoin interest rate will work is an open question. Even if the completely free market approach is adopted for Bitcoin rates, it might not even be the case that the Bitcoin interest rate would be significantly higher than the interest rates for fiat money. It could, for example, be cheaper to borrow in Bitcoin. While demand to borrow Bitcoin is low, demand to lend Bitcoin is often quite high. Because Bitcoin has a supply cap and it tends to appreciate, demand to invest and save in Bitcoin is high. Investors do not need to be encouraged by high interest rates to invest in Bitcoin, as they want exposure to an appreciating asset anyway. Therefore, perhaps Bitcoin interest rates should be very low. In Bitcoin's short history, most Bitcoin interest rates have indeed been reasonably low. However, due to a lack of sustainable demand for Bitcoin loans, it is difficult to see how this debt market will mature and what kind of interest rates we could experience in the long term.

The desired endgame for most Bitcoiners is clear, they want the free markets approach to interest rates. Many Bitcoin supporters believe in a hyperbitcoinisation type scenario, where rampant inflation causes a loss of confidence in fiat money. Bitcoin then becomes a significant store of value in the economy and some merchants begin demanding payments in Bitcoin. Bitcoin could then become a major unit of account. If this happens, some businesses may slowly start to want to take out loans in Bitcoin. Interest rates may then finally be free to some extent, perhaps for the first time in history.

In this scenario it is difficult to reason much about what kind of interest rates we would have. What levels would interest rates be? How volatile would interest rates be over time? What would the interest rate duration curve look like? What would the dispersion of rates be across different lenders and borrowers in the economy? It is unlikely we will obtain the answers to these questions by analysis or logical reasoning. We would just have to wait and see. What we can do however, is look at the story of interest rates in Bitcoin and cryptocurrency so far.

Part Two

Cryptocurrency Interest Rate History

7

The Early Years

For the first three or so years of Bitcoin, there was not much in the way of interest rates, yield or opportunities to earn a passive income. In 2011 there were a few Bitcoin mining related investment schemes, many of which turned out to be scams. Many of these schemes took place on the Global Bitcoin Stock Exchange (GBLSE), an early Bitcoin based stock exchange platform. For example, in May 2012 some mining contracts on GBLSE offered an annual rate of return of 106%. There were also non-mining investment opportunities, such as TYGRR_BANK, which promised an annual rate of return of 211%.[55] None of these schemes reached a scale that is particularly noticeable, except one, one of the highest returning savings schemes, the "Bitcoin Savings & Trust" product.

Bitcoin Savings & Trust

Bitcoin Savings & Trust launched in November 2011 and was perhaps the first example of a Bitcoin interest rate, at least related to a product that attracted a significant amount of capital. Trendon Shavers (AKA Pirate40) pseudonymously operated a ponzi scheme where he promised a return of 1% per day if you sent him Bitcoin.[56] This is an annualised rate of 3,678%. The available interest increased the more one deposited. 4.2% a week for under 100 Bitcoin, 5.6% a week for up to 500 Bitcoin and then 7% a week for over 2,000 Bitcoin. The investment scheme was said to be engaged in several trading strategies: i. Lending Bitcoin to third party network members,

---

[55] https://bitcoinmagazine.com/business/ponzi-schemes-the-danger-of-high-interest-savings-funds-1338461999
[56] https://bitcointalk.org/index.php?topic=50822.0

ii, Bitcoin arbitrage trading strategies on exchanges and iii. OTC transactions. Pirate40 is said to have claimed these activities, which were proprietary and secret, produced a yield of 10.65% per week and as such his yields were sustainable and covered by the profits. At its peak over 500,000 Bitcoin were deposited into the scheme, worth around US$7 million at the time.[57]

It is not clear whether the scheme was always a ponzi scheme. Trendon appears to have acted as an intermediary, taking client deposits and then loaning them out, possibly to traders on the largest Bitcoin exchange at the time, MtGox. These debts are likely to have gone bad resulting in insolvency. Pirate40 blamed one large debtor for this.[58] It is also possible that Pirate40 was not directly operating a ponzi scheme himself, he could have been passing client funds over to a third party, who was operating a ponzi scheme. While this may not be exactly what happened in 2022, this structure may share some characteristics with the cryptocurrency deposit taking institutions of 2022, who may have had too much exposure to large leveraged funds such as Three Arrows Capital (3AC). Anyway, at some point in 2012, Bitcoin Savings and Trust, converted from a lending operation to a ponzi scheme, where old investors were paid out with new client deposits.

On 17 August 2012, the Bitcoin Savings & Trust scheme was finally shut down and closed for new deposits. As a result, the price of Bitcoin crashed, from around US$15 a coin to US$10. Before rallying again and stabilising at around US$12. Pirate40 explained his decision to close the scheme as follows:

> *As the fund grew there were larger and larger coin movements which put strain on my reserve accounts and ultimately caused delays on [withdrawals] and the inability to fund orders within my system. On the 14th I made a final attempt to relieve pressure off the system*

---

[57] https://bitcoinmagazine.com/business/the-pirate-saga-and-so-it-ends
[58] https://bitcointalk.org/index.php?topic=101339.0

> *by reducing the rates I offered for deposits. In a perfect world this would allow me to hold more coins in reserve outside the system, but instead it only exponentially increased the amount of withdrawals overnight causing mass panic from many of my lenders.*

Despite the closure, Pirate40 still maintained at this point that all depositors would get their money back, plus interest. However, many in the community did not believe the deposits would be returned. For example, Bitcoin developer Gregory Maxwell sarcastically said to Pirate40 over IRC "since everyone assumes you're going to vanish with all the coins; why not do so?"

As it turns out, the scheme was a classic ponzi scheme and depositors did not get all their money back. Approximately 48 of the 100 investors lost all of their money. Mr Shavers was eventually arrested in 2014 and pleaded guilty in 2015. Then in 2016 he was sentenced by a judge in Manhattan to 18 months in prison for securities fraud.[59]

On 30 August 2012, Mr Shavers ironically lost a 5,000 Bitcoin bet against a critic of his service, the bet was over whether Bitcoin Savings and Trust was a ponzi scheme or not. Each party sent 5,000 Bitcoin to a third-party escrow agent. On 30 August 2012 the escrow agent said:

> *I hereby declare the bet decided, [against] Pirate40. A withdrawal request made on August 15 2012, is still outstanding as of today, which triggers default.*[60]

---

[59] https://www.justice.gov/usao-sdny/pr/texas-man-sentenced-operating-bitcoin-ponzi-scheme
[60] https://www.bloomberg.com/opinion/articles/2014-11-06/bitcoin-ponzi-schemer-lost-a-bet

8

The Emergence Of Lending Markets

Bitfinex

The first significant Bitcoin lending markets emerged on a cryptocurrency exchange called Bitfinex. The exchange was founded in 2013 and the lending markets reached a significant level by early 2014. Unlike many of the other cryptocurrency trading platforms, Bitfinex was run by people with Wall Street experience. Chief Strategy Officer Phil Potter, one of the most influential people in the company, had worked for Morgan Stanley and Bear Stearns in the 1990s before moving into FinTech.[61] In contrast, the people at other cryptocurrency exchanges typically only had experience in startups or technology companies. The other major cryptocurrency exchanges which launched before Bitfinex, such as MtGox, Coinbase, Bitstamp and Kraken, only really had spot markets, Bitfinex was the real pioneer in creating lending markets.

The lending markets here were not because there was demand for Bitcoin loans, from people who wanted to withdraw Bitcoin from the Bitfinex platform to invest Bitcoin in the economy. This was absolutely not the case. The demand for loans was because Bitfinex clients wanted to speculate on cryptocurrency prices with leverage. These traders could post collateral in the form of US Dollars, Bitcoin or Ethereum and use this balance to borrow funds in a lending market on the platform. This was a peer-to-peer lending market, where traders could lend and borrow against each other, using an aggregated

---

[61] https://www.whatbitcoindid.com/podcast/phil-potter-on-bitfinex-and-tether

open order book with central clearing and settlement. These were market driven interest rates.

An example of this lending activity would be a trader posting Bitcoin collateral to borrow US Dollars and then using those funds to acquire more Bitcoin, increasing one's exposure to Bitcoin. With many traders wanting to speculate on appreciating cryptocurrency prices, this activity became exceptionally popular. At the same time traders could earn healthy returns lending out US Dollars to these speculators. These highly innovative and transformational features benefited Bitfinex, which soon became one of the most important companies in the cryptocurrency ecosystem. Certainly the most important company with respect to price formation. Bitfinex's Bitcoin vs US Dollar pair was the most liquid instrument in the cryptocurrency space from around mid-2014 all the way until the end of 2017, with around a 40% market share.

The features Bitfinex offered may not seem especially interesting, as many traditional brokers, such as Interactive Brokers, already provided these features in traditional markets. However, it is important to appreciate that cryptocurrency prices can be exceptionally volatile. At the same time cryptocurrency markets were open 24 hours a day, 7 days a week, 365 days a year. Very different to traditional markets with set trading hours, weekends and bank holidays. Bitfinex also had to contend with the fact that chasing customers for bad debt in the cryptocurrency space was not something that was done. Bitfinex also had to deal with other complications, for instance certain traders would borrow all the US Dollars on offer, not to trade with, but to lend out again at a higher interest rate. Bitfinex therefore had to implement extra special charges on borrowers who did not use the funds to trade within 24 hours, to deter this behaviour. Therefore, ensuring the lending markets were up and running all the time, without a major failure, was a significant technical challenge.

In some periods the annualised interest rate one could earn by lending US Dollars on Bitfinex reached as high as 700%. This was picked up by media entities such as Bloomberg and these high rates played a key role in enticing new people and new money into the space. These rates were especially attractive in an environment where interest rates in the real economy were pathetically low.

> *The 29-year-old Beijing-based programmer had $440,000 on deposit at the Hong Kong bitcoin exchange Bitfinex until last week and, on good days, would wake up to find a couple thousand more dollars in his account than when he went to sleep. The earnings came from lending his dollars to traders who wanted to leverage their bets. The exchange allowed lenders like Tian to set their own rates, and he says margin traders paid as much as 700 percent [annualised] interest to borrow dollars. At times, he earned as much in one day as holders of U.S. Treasuries earn in a decade. Margin traders paid as much as 700 percent [annualised] interest to borrow dollars*[62]

It should be noted that 700% was very much the exception, not the norm. Rates did spike to 700% for a few hours, however in most periods the US Dollar lending rate was in the 20% to 60% range. Although as the following chart shows, rates were extremely unstable. It should be noted that the following chart smooths out volatility, by using daily averages. If hourly data is used, the interest rates on Bitfinex look even more volatile.

In contrast to US Dollar rates, the Bitcoin lending rates were much lower, at around 10%. However, they were still volatile with the rate often spiking up to around 150%. Demand to borrow US Dollars to increase exposure to Bitcoin was high, in contrast there was not much demand to borrow Bitcoin. This characteristic of the markets

---

[62] https://www.bloomberg.com/professional/blog/bitcoin-traders-made-700-returns-losing-millions-hack-attack/

continued into 2022. The main reason to borrow Bitcoin was when traders wanted to short Bitcoin. Bitfinex was one of the only places traders could short Bitcoin at the time.

Bitfinex US Dollar Lending Rates (Daily averages)

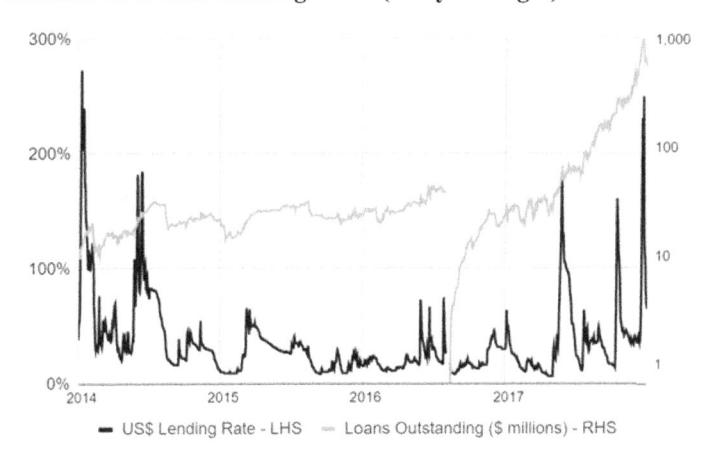

Source: bfxdata.com

Notes: Interest rate based on the daily average rate of all Bitfinex open positions, using hourly data. The right-hand axis on this chart uses a logarithmic scale, due to the strong growth in the period

The high US Dollar lending rates can be explained by several factors. The main driver was the bull market for Bitcoin in the period. Bitcoin was enjoying continued positive price momentum. This generated demand for people who wanted to borrow US Dollars to get leveraged exposure to Bitcoin. When the Bitcoin price increased further, US Dollar rates on Bitfinex sometimes rallied too. There was also a very limited supply of capital willing to lend US Dollars on Bitfinex in the 2014 to 2016 era. Not many large financial institutions were involved in the space at the time. If one wanted to lend US Dollars on Bitfinex, one had to take credit risk with the exchange. This was also not something many investors wanted to do. Who was to say the exchange wouldn't get shut down the next day, with the management team disappearing? Or what if the exchange was secretly insolvent, like MtGox was shown to be a few years earlier? For those willing to take these risks on Bitfinex, they could earn handsome returns by lending US Dollars. The epicentre of this activity, where most of the traders were based, seemed to be Hong Kong, China, Singapore, Japan and South Korea, although of course traders were based all over the world.

The fear of taking credit risk with Bitfinex was not unfounded. On 2 August 2016, Bitfinex suffered a major hack, losing around 120,000 Bitcoin, worth around US$70 million at the time (pre-hack prices). A third-party custodian company, BitGo managed some of the private keys in Bitfinex's multi-signature wallet solution at the time, and Bitfinex and BitGo have behind the scenes pointed the finger at each other for years, trying to attribute blame for the hack. To give an idea of the scale of the lending market, before the hack at the peak, US$45 million was outstanding in US Dollar loans on the platform. In contrast there were around US$14 million and US$5 million of Bitcoin and Ethereum loans outstanding respectively.

As a result of the hack Bitfinex was insolvent and withdrawals were suspended. Bitfinex then froze all positions and closed down and unwound the lending market. This is shown on the previous chart, as the outstanding loan balance declined to zero. The markets were shut down for around nine days before opening up again. To make the exchange solvent, Bitfinex then gave all customer accounts a 36% haircut, across all assets, whatever coins they held, even though only Bitcoin was stolen. Bitfinex considered only applying a haircut to those with Bitcoin in their wallets. However, due to the lending markets and the complex interrelationships between the coins, this would not have been possible and the company had to apply the haircut to all assets.

Customers were also issued a new Bitfinex token which represented the debt, the token had the ticker BFX. 80 million BFX tokens were issued, with a par value of US$1 each. This issuance was slightly higher than the hole, to provide some working capital to Bitfinex. On the first day of trading the BFX token reached a low of around 10 cents on the dollar, before ending the day at around 30 cents. At the

The Emergence Of Lending Markets 59

time there was widespread scepticism about Bitfinex's future in the cryptocurrency trading community.

Incredibly and against all odds, benefiting from the bull market and strong trading volumes, Bitfinex managed to eventually dig themselves out of the hole. A considerable number of BFX token holders had either redeemed their tokens at par value or converted the tokens into Bitfinex equity. Eventually, by around March 2017, the company had more in reserve than the tokens were worth and the company became solvent. Therefore, everyone was made whole. On the other hand many clients sold their BFX token at way below the par value and they may not feel they did well out of the hack. Some of Bitfinex's largest clients, who quite legitimately had good knowledge about Bitfinex's health and strong relationships with the Bitfinex management team, could see the strong volume going through the platform, leading to strong profits. These large clients may have acquired BFX tokens from less knowledgeable retail investors at a discount.

Amazingly, years later, in February 2022, the US Justice department indicted two individuals for possession of the stolen Bitcoin, not necessarily for actually conducting the hack itself.[63] The funds stolen by then were worth US$3.6 billion. Ilya Lichtenstein, 34, and his wife, Heather Morgan, 31 were arrested in New York. However, exactly how the hack was conducted, or if it was even these two individuals who were responsible for the hack, remains unclear.

With Bitfinex resolving its insolvency crisis, the company continued to perform well into 2017, with total US Dollar loans on the platform breaching US$1 billion by the end of the year. Rival platform Poloniex was the first major exchange to copy the lending features implemented by Bitfinex and as a result, the platform also performed well and gained market share from the more established players like Coinbase, Kraken and Bitstamp. Poloniex's more aggressive policy with respect to listing alternative coins also contributed to its growth,

---

[63] https://www.justice.gov/opa/pr/two-arrested-alleged-conspiracy-launder-45-billion-stolen-cryptocurrency

in particular Ripple and Ethereum Classic. The success of Poloniex also created the first major use case of Bitfinex's stablecoin USD Tether (USDT). Poloniex had no banking relationships and USDT was the main corridor between Bitfinex and Poloniex. Although, in this period, Bitcoin was still the main currency in the space for sending funds between exchanges and it was the primary margin and settlement currency on the trading platforms.

Bitfinex had a monumental impact on cryptocurrency trading markets and lending markets. As a result of its innovative products and astonishing survival through a crisis, cryptocurrency lending markets were born. In some form or another, they have stayed with us ever since.

The Basis Trade

In finance, the basis is the difference between the spot price of a commodity and the futures price. A market is in contango when the futures price is higher than the spot price. In contrast, backwardation is when the futures price is lower than the spot price. Bitcoin is typically in contango, as most traders in the space want to be long and expect the price to increase. Traders can use this spread to their advantage, by buying Bitcoin in the spot market and selling the future. As time progresses, towards the future's expiration date, this gap should close. The trader here should earn a profit, a type of yield or return. This can also be thought of as an interest rate. Basis risk is the risk that the price gap between the spot price and the futures price changes, as in the effective interest rate changes, due to a shift in the shape of the futures curve.

The first Bitcoin futures market was called ICBIT, which launched in 2011.[64] These first Bitcoin futures products launched in 2012.[65] The Bitcoin contract was quoted in US Dollars, settled in Bitcoin and had a duration of six months. However, this very basic platform was

---
[64] https://bitcointalk.org/index.php?topic=50817.0
[65] https://web.archive.org/web/20121110105237/https://icbit.se/node/3

difficult to use and never gained significant traction. In 2012, ICBIT explained the rationale for their Bitcoin futures products as follows:

> *Miners, merchants who accept payment in Bitcoins, or just anyone having Bitcoins who wants independence of BTC vs USD rate. This is the most typical use case for futures. Example: Miner has mined 1000 BTC and current exchange rate is $6 for 1 BTC (so marking to market that's $6000 value in Bitcoins). If rate decreases to $3 for 1 BTC by December, miner would effectively [lose] half of his money (because he needs to do certain payments in USD). To fix this problem the miner sells 600 December BTCUSD futures contract at 6.0000 price. Traders who want to speculate on the Bitcoin to fiat money rate. Buying/selling futures contracts is significantly cheaper than trading on the spot market. Also trader[s are] allowed to take any position he likes - long or short, without the need to own the corresponding currency (e.g. USD to go long in BTC, and BTC to sell for going short in BTC). Accessible leverage varies according to the specific instrument, however a rough estimate for BTCUSD contract would be close to 1:10.*

ICBIT reached its peak popularity in around 2013, before Bitfinex took over. In that period, one could earn an annualised rate of around 200% conducting the basis trade on ICBIT.[66] From around 2014 onwards, new players entered the market. Huobi, OkCoin, BTC China and BitMEX, all based in China or Hong Kong, launched Bitcoin futures contracts, based on ICBIT's design. The main innovation these new players brought to the market was the socialised loss and insurance fund system. These were pools of funds, built up inside the platform, to help pay for the winning traders when losing traders went bankrupt. These systems greatly improved the reliability of the trading platforms.

---

[66] https://blog.bitmex.com/comeback/

From around 2018 onwards, cryptocurrency futures contracts, mostly for Bitcoin and Ethereum, finally started to gain significant traction in the market. By this time, they were available on platforms such as Binance, FTX, Bitfinex, Bybit, BitMEX and OKCoin/OKX. At the end of 2017, the world's largest traditional derivatives exchange, the Chicago Mercantile Exchange (CME), also launched Bitcoin futures. This proved to be a very successful product.

These Bitcoin and Ethereum futures contracts were used by speculators, sophisticated proprietary trading shops and hedge funds. During periods of the retail mania there was a huge flow of retail money into the market. This occurred to an incredible extent during 2021, as a result the futures tended to trade at significant premiums to the spot markets.

In April 2021 open interest in Bitcoin futures across the major platforms reached almost US$30 billion, whilst the Ethereum peak, a few months later in November 2021, reached almost US$15 billion.[67] Effective annualised Bitcoin basis rates of up to 35% could be earned at the peak in March 2021 on the native cryptocurrency platforms.[68] While on the CME, at the peak in March one could earn 16%. This arbitrage trade was essentially risk free, as long as you had the capital to keep your position open, you were patient enough to wait for the futures expiration date and the exchange remained solvent. These high rates of return reflected the fact that most participants in cryptocurrency trading markets expected the underlying prices of the coins to keep on increasing. At the time of writing, in October 2022, these annualised futures basis rates are more moderate, at around 2%. However, while annualised futures basis rates were very important rates in the cryptocurrency space, they are not really interest rates, because they are not really charged to a borrower.

---

[67] https://www.theblock.co/data/crypto-markets/futures
[68] https://cointelegraph.com/news/bitcoin-futures-premium-hits-30-but-analyst-says-this-time-it-s-different

BitMEX

BitMEX is a cryptocurrency derivatives trading platform, founded in 2014, by Arthur Hayes, Ben Delo and Sam Reed. BitMEX developed and offered a ground breaking new product in the industry, a perpetual swap contract, which is basically a Bitcoin futures contract that did not have an expiration date.

Unlike Bitfinex, BitMEX did not have a spot exchange nor did BitMEX have lending markets. Instead, on BitMEX, traders would deposit Bitcoin and use Bitcoin as the margin and settlement currency to trade cryptocurrency derivatives. These contracts would allow traders to open large notional positions while only having a small amount of capital in the account. For example, BitMEX allows traders to achieve effective leverage of up to 100 times, in that one could deposit 1 Bitcoin and open a position in a contract with a notional size of 100 Bitcoin.

BitMEX had to ensure its rolling swap contract effectively tracked the spot price of Bitcoin, unlike a future which tends to trade at a premium. In order to achieve this there was something called a funding rate associated with the contract. Unlike futures with an expiry date and settlement, there is no basis rate. Instead, BitMEX used a funding rate, which was initially associated with the cost of borrowing the underlying asset on Bitfinex. This interest rate is charged to traders or received by traders, depending on if they are long or short. This mechanism mimics how the margin lending worked on Bitfinex, with traders exchanging interest payments between each other.

At first BitMEX used the Bitfinex Bitcoin and US Dollar lending rates to calculate the funding rate. The rate was the cost to borrow US Dollars on Bitfinex minus the cost to borrow Bitcoin. As explained above, this number was almost always positive. If a BitMEX client went long Bitcoin, they would pay this rate, while if they went short Bitcoin, they would receive this interest rate. Therefore, if demand to go long Bitcoin increased on Bitfinex, the rate would be higher and it would be more expensive to go long on BitMEX. The idea behind this seems somewhat related to a retail instrument in traditional finance, CFDs (Contract For Difference). These contracts typically have no expiry and longs pay a funding rate overnight to shorts, depending on the base rate of the currency in question. However, each CFD only has one leverage rate, while BitMEX wanted one highly liquid uniform contract across all leverage ratios.

BitMEX's funding rate did not work particularly effectively. The issue was that Bitfinex traders were using around 3x leverage, while BitMEX supported up to 100x. Therefore, the interest rate was too low, as it reflected demand from traders using 3x, while the traders were actually using higher leverage. At the same time, the trade flow on BitMEX was more speculative. Therefore, BitMEX changed the methodology of the contract, adding a new component to the funding rate calculation. BitMEX looked at the price of the perpetual swap contract in the last period (now using 8 hour windows) and compared it to the funding rate adjusted spot price of the underlying asset over the same period, using data from the spot exchanges such as Bitfinex. If the perpetual contract was trading at a larger premium to the underlying than the funding rate, traders going long the contract would make greater payments to those going short in the next period, and vice versa. This mechanism helped ensure the price of the contract closely followed the spot price. This mechanism proved to be highly effective.

It is not clear if this rate represents a Bitcoin interest rate. It can be thought of as a special mechanism used by a trading platform to achieve a particular objective, rather than an interest rate. This was certainly less of an interest rate than even the borrow rates on Bitfinex, which were more linked to actual loans and debt. Even if the debt could only be used to speculate.

This new type of derivative contract meant that traders could achieve the desired amount of leverage without using spot margin trading and lending markets. BitMEX made the ability to obtain leveraged exposure to Bitcoin even easier than on Bitfinex. As a result of this, from mid-2017 onwards, BitMEX enjoyed strong growth. By 2018 the perpetual swap contract was doing billions of US Dollars per day in notional trading volume. This new derivative contract type eventually took over from Bitfinex's Bitcoin market as the most liquid instrument in the space and as a result, Bitfinex's lending market rates became slightly less significant. In around 2020 BitMEX lost its crown as having the most traded Bitcoin contract, as other exchanges like Binance and FTX became the market leaders. However, these other platforms copied BitMEX's perpetual swap contract innovation, and the perpetual contract remains extremely popular to this day. Whether it's an interest rate or not, the funding rate for this contract remains one of the most important quasi Bitcoin rates.

9

Bitcoin As Collateral

Towards the end of 2017, the idea of using Bitcoin as collateral to borrow US Dollars gained some traction. The rationale for this was that many people had become wealthy due to Bitcoin price appreciation and they may want to use that wealth to buy goods and services, for example a home, a car or a yacht. These individuals may want to retain their Bitcoin holdings and therefore they can use the Bitcoin as collateral to borrow US Dollars and avoid selling Bitcoin. This meant the lender didn't need to do any credit checks as they had a highly liquid form of collateral instead, Bitcoin, which was posted with the lender. The borrower also had the advantage of not realising a capital gain by selling the Bitcoin, therefore they may have avoided or deferred taxation.

This type of structure is similar to the services investment banks provide some wealthy clients. For instance, a successful founder of a company may want to purchase a luxury home, something they can afford due to the success of their startup. However, they may not want to sell shares in their company, because they want to retain control, retain the economic upside and avoid capital gains tax. Therefore, they could place the shares of their company as collateral with the private wealth division of a large investment bank such as UBS or Morgan Stanley. The investment bank will then provide the company founder with the liquidity they need to purchase anything they want, whenever they need it. This service is very common in traditional investment banking and people began to see that there was some merit in applying it to Bitcoin and cryptocurrency. Several companies were founded based on this idea.

Blockfi

BlockFi is a New York based firm, founded in 2017, which provided cryptocurrency backed loans.[69] BlockFi is believed to be the first company to provide such loans as a business, where the funds were supposed to be withdrawn from the platform. The first loan was provided in January 2018, where BlockFi lent out fiat money, while cryptocurrency was provided as collateral. Customers could deposit Bitcoin, use it as collateral and then borrow US Dollars. The US Dollars were paid to clients via a wire transfer. In February 2018, the loans would work as follows:

- The customer deposits Bitcoin or Ethereum with BlockFi.
- The customer can borrow US Dollars, paying an annual interest rate of 12%.
- An origination fee of 1%.
- The loan could be up to 40% of the value of Bitcoin deposited or in the case of Ethereum, only 35%, due to the higher volatility of Ethereum. This is called an initial margin.
- If the cryptocurrency price fell, such that the loan to value ratio increased to 70% and the client did not add more equity to the position, the client could get liquidated. This is the maintenance margin.[70]

As for the Bitcoin and Ethereum BlockFi received, it was initially just stored in company wallets. The funds were not lent out or rehypothecated. They were just stored safely, ready to pay back the customers should they repay the loans and withdraw. The 12% interest rate was high enough and BlockFi did not need to earn more money by lending out the Bitcoin. On the other hand, BlockFi was very much growth focused, it had the culture of a VC backed American technology startup, rather than one focused on what some

---

[69] https://bitcoinmagazine.com/business/after-4m-funding-round-blockfi-eyes-savings-account-crypto-credit-cards
[70] https://web.archive.org/web/20180201092502/https://blockfi.com/

consider as "Bitcoin principles" of security, resilience and protection in a financial crisis.

Ledn

The next crypto currency collateralised lending platform to launch was Ledn, in Toronto Canada, which was founded in August 2018. This was essentially the Canadian equivalent of BlockFi. In February 2019, Ledn charged a rate of 12% to borrow Canadian dollars,[71] a rate identical to BlockFi in the United States.

Initially, just like at BlockFi, the company did nothing with the Bitcoin deposited by the clients. The users could see the unmoved transaction outputs on the Bitcoin blockchain, such that they knew the Bitcoin was safely sitting there. In contrast to BlockFi's growth culture, Ledn seemed a bit more in tune to the aforementioned so-called Bitcoin values.

Unchained Capital

Unchained Capital is another company which offers US Dollar loans based on Bitcoin collateral. The company was founded in 2016 and exclusively provides Bitcoin related services, such as facilitating Bitcoin purchases and storing Bitcoin in a multi-signature wallet on behalf of their customers. The company also provides US Dollar loans with Bitcoin as collateral.

Unchained Capital was and still is, the most conservative of the three lenders. The company has never and still does not, loan out or otherwise rehypothecate customer Bitcoin. The customer Bitcoin is always stored inside the company's multi-signature wallet system. The company still provides this lending service today, charging an interest rate of between 12% to 16% on US Dollar loans, with an origination fee of 1%.

---

[71] https://web.archive.org/web/20190226000516/https://ledn.io/

10

Bitcoin's Risk Free Rate

The traditional pre-cryptocurrency system has a concept of the risk free rate of return, the return you get from holding government bonds. This interest rate should in theory be lower than all other rates in the economy, which have higher risks. Nobody should lend to a company or individual at a rate lower than the risk free rate. There is a similar idea in Bitcoin, in that you can earn risk free money in some protocols, which could be a floor on interest rates in the cryptocurrency-system. However, these are not totally risk free, they are in theory only counterparty risk free. You can still lose money in other ways, for example by getting hacked.

The Lightning Network Rate

The first and most obvious example of a possible risk free rate in Bitcoin, is providing liquidity in the lightning network. Assuming one runs their own lightning node, there is no custodial relationship with a third party and one can earn lightning network routing fee income. This income is therefore counterparty risk free. However, one needs to have their private key on an exposed online machine and therefore there are risks. For example, the risk that your machine gets hacked and the funds get stolen. There is also the risk that your machine goes offline for an extended period and as a result, you could lose money.

The lightning network is a network of interconnected peer-to-peer payment channels. Instead of using the blockchain to make payments, senders and receivers need to find a path with sufficient liquidity along these non-custodial channels. Only in the event of a bad actor should the Bitcoin blockchain be used as a dispute resolution service. Lightning has several advantages over on-chain Bitcoin payments, namely: lower fees, greater privacy and speed.

One of the main problems with the lightning network is finding a path with enough liquidity to make payments. This makes lightning potentially unsuitable for very large payments. On the other hand, since those who provide liquidity receive routing fees, an equilibrium fee level should be obtained, where there is sufficient liquidity, at a price.

To provide liquidity, all one needs to do is provide capital (in the form of Bitcoin) and run a lightning node. Some users have reported earning an annual yield of up to 1%.[72] Other more expert users have been able to earn even higher rates of return. These are very much variable interest rates, not stable fixed income type returns. If the lightning network becomes popular, one can imagine the kind of economics which could apply. For instance, if other forms of Bitcoin interest rates increase, for example the basis trade premium, lightning network fees may need to increase to compensate investors more for choosing to provide liquidity on the lightning network. Therefore, in a bull market, where futures trade at a large premium over the spot market, lightning fees could be structurally higher.

However, there is no one lightning network interest rate, available for all liquidity providers. Most lightning node implementations have features in place, which will open channels for users and automatically provide liquidity and earn fees. However, the returns from using these are far lower than what is available to the experts who actively manage and rebalance their channels, to maximise the yield. This involves analysing the lightning network, assessing the payment flows and constantly balancing one's channels. Alex Bosworth is a lightning network developer who is perhaps considered

---

[72] https://blog.bitmex.com/the-lightning-network-part-2-routing-fee-economics/

as the leading expert in this field. He disclosed that in the first half of 2021 he made US$30,000 in lightning network fees.[73]

Due to how challenging earning a decent yield is, perhaps this rate should not be considered an interest rate. Again, perhaps Proudhon's 1849 argument that interest is a "reward for idleness" is not applicable here. At least so far in the lightning network, earning a decent yield requires hard work.

Lightning Channel Marketplaces

Lightning channel marketplaces started to emerge in 2021 and 2022. The idea is that merchants accepting lightning payments will need liquidity and can pay liquidity providers to open channels with them. Marketplaces have therefore emerged, where merchants and liquidity providers come together and exchange cash for liquidity.

Lightning Labs, a key lightning network infrastructure company, developed a service called Lightning Pool. While a startup called Amboss also provides a relatively similar service called Magma. Both these marketplaces are non-custodial. Lightning Pool is designed to aggregate demand and supply for liquidity into a pool and there is an auction process which determines the price of liquidity. Magma is a slightly newer service and at the time of writing is just under one year old. In contrast to Lightning Pool, Magma has more of a peer-to-peer type structure, where entities who desire liquidity can choose the individual liquidity provider they want. The advantage of the Magma structure is that it is easier to select who provides the liquidity. Some liquidity providers are more reliable than others and therefore being able to more easily choose who provides the liquidity has clear benefits. On the other hand, the potential advantages of Lightning Pool are that it could offer better liquidity and it can be more automated.

---

[73] https://twitter.com/alexbosworth/status/1421156957977710596

Magma provides a marketplace which displays the offers (Size and interest rate) and ranks liquidity providers with a reputation score, based on their reliability. Once the liquidity provider is selected, they are paid a fee and open a lightning channel with the buyer. Amboss also publishes average annual yield information on their website. This is the annualised cost to a merchant of buying liquidity as a proportion of the liquidity they receive. At the time of writing, Amboss' website indicates the average yield based on this metric is 3.27%, based on 46 Bitcoin of deployed liquidity in the history of Magma. Based on data provided by the Amboss team, historically average weekly interest rates peaked at 15% and were reasonably volatile during the first 30 weeks of the service. Since then, rates have settled down and are flattish at around 2.5% to 3.0%.

When purchasing liquidity on Magma the buyer can select the duration they desire and therefore a yield curve can be constructed, based on these different durations. The longest duration available is around six months. Based on historical data, the interest rate declines the longer the duration. This is the opposite of what one observes in a traditional bond market, where longer duration instruments typically have higher yields. The reason for this is that the liquidity provider could withdraw funds from the channel early and therefore the provision of liquidity is not guaranteed. If they do this their reputation will be damaged, but they may still earn the interest income. This risk is reflected in the price. Therefore, although one needs to pay higher absolute fees for longer duration liquidity, annualised yields decline the longer the duration of the deal is.

Due to the length of the duration here, the income in these marketplaces could be more passive than using the lightning network directly to earn routing fees. Therefore, it is possible the market for lightning channels could represent a non-custodial risk free Bitcoin rate of return. However, even this market requires some active management and it should not really be classified as passive income. The market size here is currently very small, Magma has done around 46 Bitcoin of volume and Lightning Pool is around twice that. This is not especially significant in the grand scheme of things, however, it is of course possible that usage of the lightning network grows and these rates become more economically significant.

CoinJoin

CoinJoin is a method of improving privacy when using Bitcoin. More concisely, when spending Bitcoin one cooperates with other users and combines outputs from multiple senders into one transaction. That way it may be much more challenging for anyone analysing the blockchain to determine the flow of funds. If one wants to use this method today, there are essentially two choices: JoinMarket or Wasabi Wallet. Each of these options is a piece of software with a Bitcoin wallet and separate peer-to-peer network like functionality, such that the wallet can cooperate with other user's wallets, to combine the spending. The implementation we will talk about here is JoinMarket, as a counterparty risk free yield is available. JoinMarket has something called a "yield generator bot", providing another potential risk free rate. Wasabi Wallet does not appear to have an equivalent feature.

If one wants to use CoinJoin to anonymise one's coins and achieve stronger privacy, you need to find other peers willing to mix coins with you. However, there may not always be matching demand from somebody else. Different users may have different time preferences with respect to how quickly they want to achieve strong privacy. A user in a rush can either wait for a potentially considerable amount of time or pay somebody else a fee to incentivise them to mix with you. These fees are somewhat analogous to lightning routing fees, in lightning you are paying for somebody else's liquidity, the equivalent in CoinJoin is that you may also need to pay for somebody else's liquidity, such that you can mix your coins with them. There is therefore an opportunity for the other side of the privacy trade, the maker, to earn a yield. The JoinMarket Wiki describes the yield generator bot as follows:

> *Being a market maker allows holders of bitcoin to collect fees. With this, the Yield Generator script is used to earn an income from long-term held bitcoin. The investment is very low risk as the software only signs transactions that are valid and pay operators the correct amount in coinjoin fees. Although the coins must be held on an online hot wallet. The investment has no commitment as bitcoins can be withdrawn at any time. It also improves the privacy of the held bitcoins as well as privacy and fungibility in the entire ecosystem, which makes bitcoin as a currency more useful and thus increases its value.[74]*

According to bitcoinkpis.com[75] it appears as if around 2,000 Bitcoin per week flowed through JoinMarket in 2022, although the volume is very volatile, week to week. At current Bitcoin prices this represents around US$2 billion per year in volume. This volume does appear to be quite significant and it has been growing. At the same time, unlike almost every other metric in the ecosystem, it does not appear to be driven by the Bitcoin price, perhaps demonstrating more fundamental non-speculative growth.

One should look at the US$2 billion per annum number with caution however, this may be the same money flowing through JoinMarket multiple times. This is still very much a niche activity and it may not be especially economically significant. In late 2022, there are perhaps around 4,000 Bitcoin at any one time, waiting to participate in on JoinMarket. At the same time, large pools of capital, such as institutional money may not be able to participate in providing privacy liquidity due to regulatory concerns.

As for the magnitudes of the yields one can potentially earn, these are quite low. One can expect to earn an annualised rate of between 1% to 2%, although this variable rate is very volatile. You can earn an

---

[74] https://en.bitcoin.it/wiki/JoinMarket#Yield_generator
[75] http://www.bitcoinkpis.com/privacy

annual rate of up to 4% in some periods when demand to mix is strong. These rates do not appear particularly recklessly high and may be quite moderate, for an asset like Bitcoin, which has low inflation and a known final supply cap. JoinMarket could therefore be an attractive option for long term holders looking for counterparty risk free returns. On the other hand, it is technically quite complicated to set up and it does expose the coins to the risk of hacking, as it requires the private keys to be in an online wallet.

Just like with the lightning network, it is possible that usage of the JoinMarket system becomes influenced by the economic cycle. It is possible that in the future, if interest rates rise, privacy becomes more expensive and if interest rates decline, yield hungry privacy liquidity providers may make privacy cheaper. Although the regulatory uncertainty of these privacy systems could dampen the impact here, because capital from certain sources cannot easily flow into privacy systems.

These JoinMarket yields do genuinely appear to be a type of passive income, in that once you have your JoinMarket client set up properly, you can passively leave it on for months on end and earn a yield, without active management and involvement. This is somewhat different from lightning, which requires more active work. Therefore, JoinMarket perhaps offers more of a genuine candidate than lightning for Bitcoin's risk free rate. Being a maker on JoinMarket is more of a financial type activity than an operating business. However, it would need to grow considerably from the current levels to be significant. For now, both the lightning network and JoinMarket are somewhat segregated from the more speculative, trading driven rates in the ecosystem, which are much more significant. How this may change over time depends on one's view of the cryptocurrency space. It is possible that the space becomes less speculative and trader driven over time and this privacy related quasi-interest rate gains in significance. For now though, this seems a little farfetched.

11

The Earn Model

BlockFi's Earn Pivot

In March 2019 BlockFi rolled out a new feature: interest bearing cryptocurrency deposits. This is often referred to as the "earn" model, a way to attract retail deposits. As the project launched, a client could deposit Bitcoin and earn a yield of 6.2%.[76] This was a variable interest rate and BlockFi reserved the right to change the interest rate at any point in time. When questioned about the interest rate in 2019, the BlockFi CEO, Zac Prince, described the rate as a "loss leader". Prince went on to say:

> *We believe that we will be able to continue raising venture capital supporting the growth and at a certain point down the road [when] we're a much bigger company, maybe we're a public company, then we can say: 'Ok, we turn to profit now.' We anticipate being able to raise larger and larger amounts of venture capital for a while, at least for the next couple of years.*

Mr Prince was considered a darling of the VC firms. He thought like them and said what they wanted to hear. Growth was the priority, not generating cash flow, profitability or sustainability. BlockFi generated significant losses due to this strategy. In 2020 the company made a gross loss of US$5 million on US$64 million of revenue.[77]

---

[76] https://www.coindesk.com/markets/2019/03/20/25-million-in-2-weeks-blockfi-booms-as-bitcoin-and-ether-investors-seek-interest/
[77] https://twitter.com/blane9171/status/1537371790376312833/photo/1

This loss was due to negative interest spreads, designed to attract customers, grow and build market share. When including administrative and other costs, the company generated US$63 million in operating losses in 2020. In 2021, a year of massive cryptocurrency price appreciation and flows into the space, the company did generate a gross profit, however the operating loss was even larger. The operating loss in 2021was US$222 million, on the back of US$101 million in staff costs, US$45 million in marketing costs and amazingly US$37 million in Ethereum gas fees (transaction fees). This growing cost base was to facilitate the huge growth, which was expected to continue. In 2021, client assets generating a yield increased by 125% to US$9.9 billion and BlockFi's headcount soared 121% to 818 people. This was clearly following the playbook BlockFi's investors wanted. In a period of such low interest rates and cheap money, they were happy to keep financing the losses as long as the company was growing and future fundings rounds at higher valuations were on the cards.

The theory that BlockFi did not need profits early on as investors could finance the growth was proved correct. Venture funding appeared incredibly easy to obtain. According to Crunchbase,[78] BlockFi was able to raise:

- US$50m in a debt round in July 2018,
- US$4m in a convertible note in December 2018,
- A venture round in January 2019,
- An US$18.3m Series A round in August 2019,
- A US$30m Series B round in February 2020,
- A US$50m Series C round in August 2020,
- A US$350m Series D round in February 2021 at a US$3 billion valuation, and,
- A US$500m Series E round in August 2021 at a US$4.5 billion valuation.

---

[78] https://www.crunchbase.com/organization/blockfi-inc/investor_financials

This represents total funding of US$1 billion. Investors included Bain Capital, Tiger Global, Susquehanna Government Products, Peter Thiel, Jump Capital, Castle Island Ventures, Three Arrows Capital (3AC), Galaxy Digital, Coinbase Ventures and Paradigm.[79] [80] [81] A who's who of some of the most respected VC firms in the world including the biggest cryptocurrency VC firms.

This growth model often works in the technology sector, when backing the clear leader such as AirBNB or Uber, or even Amazon. These companies can operate at a loss for years, building their dominance and only then do they raise prices and generate profits. This is probably what the VC investors had in mind. However, it is not clear if this aggressive growth at all costs plan always works. Particularly in the financial services industry, when lending is involved. At the same time BlockFi was not especially dominant. There were other competitors and it did not seem logical that this lending and banking business model had a winner takes all network effect dynamic, which applies in other areas. If BlockFi won customers by offering unsustainably high returns for a period of time, these customers would not necessarily remain captive to BlockFi, unlike AirBNB or Uber where there is a large pool of service providers.

BlockFi kept the yield on Bitcoin deposits at this 6% level for several years and this did attract a considerable number of customers and a large amount of capital. 6% was far above the base rate one could earn with US Dollars. In theory, Bitcoin should have low interest rates, as there is very little real fundamental demand to borrow Bitcoin. With its robust supply cap, Bitcoin is a strong asset and does not require high yields to attract investors. Especially in an environment where the base US Dollar rate in the economy was almost 0%. The 6% Bitcoin deposit rate may therefore have been too high and unsustainable. Paying a rate like this for so long probably

---

[79] https://blockfi.com/investors/
[80] https://techcrunch.com/2021/03/11/blockfi-lands-a-350m-series-d-at-3b-valuation-for-its-fast-growing-crypto-lending-platform/
[81] https://www.forbes.com/sites/robertanzalone/2020/04/09/three-arrows-capital-invests-in-blockfi-after-its-series-b-round

meant BlockFi was operating with negative interest spreads, at least with respect to this product.

BlockFi also started paying interest on US Dollar stablecoin deposits. These interest rates tended to be much higher than the rates with Bitcoin or Ethereum. This is primarily because there was more demand to borrow US Dollar stablecoins and this greater demand drove up the potential returns that BlockFi could earn by lending out the US Dollars. From the point of view of the lender, it is also somewhat logical that an inflationary currency (The US Dollar) should produce higher yields than a currency with a fixed supply like Bitcoin, where most users expect its value to appreciate. To be encouraged to invest in US Dollars, one needs to be enticed with a higher yield. The US Dollar stablecoin yields may also have been too high, as they were far in excess of what traditional banks paid in the period (essentially zero). The rates may therefore have indicated that BlockFi was taking excessive risks in order to obtain these yields. Risks that the customers may not have been aware of.

However, BlockFi did implement caps on the high rates, at least with respect to Bitcoin. In July 2020 the retail interest rates BlockFi offered were as follows:

BlockFi Earn Rates - July 2020

Currency	Amount	Annual Rate
Bitcoin	0 - 5	6%
Bitcoin	> 5	3.2%
Ethereum	> 0	4.5%
Litecoin	> 0	3.8%
USDC	> 0	8.6%

Source: https://web.archive.org/web/20200609062720/https://blockfi.com/rates/
Note: USDC is a custodial US Dollar stablecoin provided by Circle

While BlockFi's earn business was growing, the interest rates in its collateralised cryptocurrency lending business were also coming down. At launch the rate BlockFi lent out money was 12%, by June 2020 this had fallen to 9.75% with a 50% loan to value ratio, or only 4.5% with a 20% loan to value ratio. This 4.5% rate is a negative spread compared to the unsustainable 6% Bitcoin deposit rate on offer.

There were obviously some synergies between the cryptocurrency lending business and the earn business. Interest payments from the lending business could pay for the interest costs on the earn side of the business. Very much the idea of a simple banking model, with customer loans funding deposit interest payments. However, the earn business grew much faster than the lending business. This therefore meant customer funds were no longer just safely stored, they were now leant out to other counterparties. This applied to both sides of the business, on the earn side and the lending side, customer funds were lent out. The counterparties included proprietary trading firms, market makers and other financial entities. This was necessary in order to try and earn a yield to pay the customers the rates they desired.

While there was some retail demand to borrow US Dollars, retail demand to borrow Bitcoin was extremely low. On the other hand, some traders, proprietary trading shops and market makers did want to borrow Bitcoin. They needed Bitcoin to deploy on trading platforms such as BitMEX and move funds between cryptocurrency exchanges. These firms often did not want exposure to Bitcoin, but just wanted to use it to earn returns, deploying, for example, quantitative trading strategies they had developed in the traditional financial world into the cryptocurrency ecosystem.

BlockFi's high earn rates persisted all the way until the summer of 2021, when the highest Bitcoin rate was lowered from 6% to 4%. At this point Bitcoin balances over five Bitcoin earned just 0.25%. The US Dollar rates also declined. Tiers were introduced for US Dollars and the highest rate went from 8.6% to 7.5%. For balances over US$50,000 the interest rate was 5%. By October 2021, BlockFi increased the Bitcoin rate slightly, to 4.5%, but lowered the cap to just 0.1 Bitcoin. Balances above 0.35 Bitcoin received just 0.1%. These Bitcoin and US Dollar rates persisted into 2022.

Ledn's Pivot

As BlockFi lent out customer funds, they were able to offer more competitive interest rates. These superior rates helped BlockFi win market share from competitors such as Ledn. The Ledn founders asked some of their clients what they wanted: more competitive interest rates or to stick with the model of no rehypothecation. Perhaps unsurprisingly, clients chose the more competitive interest rates and Ledn started deploying client capital, although it must be said, in a much more cautious manner than BlockFi. Only Unchained Capital remained stubborn with its ultra conservative no rehypothecation stance. Ledn also adopted the earn model, something Unchained Capital never engaged in.

From 2020 onwards, there were also several other notable changes in the collateralised cryptocurrency lending industry. The lenders stopped using bank wires to send US Dollars to their clients. Instead, customers required US Dollar stablecoins. This may indicate the success, adoption and better user experience of the stablecoins. On the other hand, it could indicate that customers were no longer using the funds in the real world, to purchase things like cars and houses. It could indicate that customers were keeping the funds inside the cryptocurrency ecosystem, perhaps to speculate. Indeed, Ledn noticed that many clients would do what they called a "deposit cycle". An example of this is as follows: A customer has 1 Bitcoin and uses it to borrow US Dollars at a 50% loan to value ratio. The customer then takes this 0.5 Bitcoin worth of US Dollar stablecoin and purchases more Bitcoin with it. This Bitcoin is then deposited back at Ledn and used again to borrow 0.25 Bitcoin worth of US Dollars. The customers were now using the cryptocurrency lending platforms to increase their exposure to rising cryptocurrency prices in a bull market, not to buy houses and avoid capital gains taxes. After Ledn spotted this customer behaviour, they then automated the whole process, allowing borrowers to obtain a 100% loan to value ratio product.

Maple

There is one more lending company worth mentioning, one marketing itself as a DeFi protocol, a project called Maple. Maple adopted the earn business model of BlockFi, attracting cryptocurrency deposits and lending it to proprietary trading firms. However, Maple was based on DeFi, rather than being a centralised company. What this essentially means is that customers deposit funds, typically in the form of USDC, to an Ethereum smart contract rather than a central entity. This contract was still effectively controlled by the Maple organisation, therefore the argument that Maple is DeFi based is a bit flimsy. It is mostly a centralised company just like BlockFi, with smart contracts used to improve transparency. In addition to the normal yield, users were also rewarded with Maple's native token, this supplemented the yield and allowed the company to advertise a higher rate of return.

The key differentiator between Maple and the other earn businesses was transparency. With Maple you could see exactly what happened to your money. The USDC you provided was lent out in a pool to a number of proprietary trading firms and on Maple's website all the details of the loans were provided. These details included the counterparty, the loan value, any collateral they provided (typically Bitcoin or Ethereum), the loan duration and the interest rate. The counterparties included many of the top trading shops and market makers in the space, including Alameda Research, Wintermute, Amber Group, FBG Capital, GSR and BlockTower. These companies typically borrow at 10% to 15%. Lenders typically earned around 9% or 16%, when including the Maple token rewards.

According to maple.finance, at the time of writing in October 2022, around US$1.9 billion of loans have originated on the platform and the current outstanding balance is US$322 million. The peak balance of outstanding loans was around US$1 billion. Although this is a significant decline since the booming market of 2021, the loan book performed reasonably well, with only one major default of around US$10 million.

The key point here is that Maple's more fully transparent model appears superior to the model adopted by BlockFi and the other centralised earn companies. If you are going to lend US Dollars to a group of cryptocurrency proprietary trading houses, which may be risky in certain economic climates, it's probably better to make that clear to the lender, rather than trying to frame it a bit like a bank deposit.

New Players Join The Game

In 2021, with the earn model proving itself to be a huge success, in terms of asset growth at least, a whole host of new companies joined the game, providing the same services. With interest rates in the real economy suppressed to dangerously low levels, the recklessly high yields inside the cryptocurrency ecosystem appeared exceptionally attractive. This caused a huge flow of both retail and institutional money into the space. These investors were both keen to earn the attractive yields and also to obtain leveraged upside to increasing cryptocurrency prices in the bull market. Eager to capitalise on the flow and excitement of the space, many other companies entered, adopting the earn model.

In April 2021, leading Bitcoin researcher and engineer, Jameson Lopp evaluated the leading earn model companies. The companies are listed, with their respective Bitcoin interest rates, in the following table.

Bitcoin Interest Rate Offered to Depositors - April 2021

Platform	Bitcoin Interest Rate
Abra	4.5%
BitLeague	5.8% - 9%
BlockFi	6% (Max 0.5 BTC)
Celsius	3.5%
CoinLoan	5.2%
Crypto.com	1.5% - 4.5%
Hodlnaut	6.2%
Ledn	6.15% (Max 2 BTC)
Luno	4%
Midas	17%
MyConstant	4% - 7%
Nexo	4% - 7%
Vauld	6.7%
Voyager	6.25%
Youhodler	4.8%

Source: https://blog.lopp.net/custodial-bitcoin-yield-generator-testing/

12

Stablecoins

From around 2018 to 2020, US Dollar stablecoins took over as the main settlement currency and trading pair coin in the cryptocurrency trading space, replacing Bitcoin. These stablecoins also took over as the main bridge between the cryptocurrency trading platforms. As a result of this, demand to use the Bitcoin blockchain declined and Bitcoin transaction fees therefore also declined from their 2017 peak. This was an era of unprecedented growth and success for blockchain based US Dollar stablecoins. There are several reasons this success:

- **Stability** - The primary reason is the obvious one, stability. Proprietary trading firms and market makers would rather have their working capital in US Dollars than a more volatile currency like Bitcoin.

- **Trading Pairs** - The trading platforms used the stablecoin US Dollar Tether (USDT) as the main trading pair against the crypto-tokens, rather than Bitcoin. This was simply more user friendly. For example, traders think about the price of Ethereum in US Dollars. They want to bet the price of Ethereum climbs from US$2,000 to US$4,000. Traders don't think in terms of the Ethereum price being 0.07 Bitcoin.

- **Regulatory arbitrage** - While stablecoin issuers have censored some transactions and do have this ability, by and large, most of the time, major stablecoins like USDT and USDC have the same censorship resistance characteristics of Bitcoin. All one needs to do is generate a public private key pair and one can receive and spend USDT, in the same way as Bitcoin. Therefore, getting an exchange or trading firm set up to use USDT is easy, complex and expensive banking and regulatory relationships can be avoided. Of course, it's possible that eventually regulators crack down and one day this changes, forcing some people back into Bitcoin, but for now USDT is attractive. For most traders USDT is better than Bitcoin, at least until it isn't.

- **Multi-chain** - The stablecoins can exist on multiple blockchains. This means that USDT can be sent around for low fees on Tron and one can use USDT to interact with smart contracts on Ethereum. Of course, custodial Bitcoin can also exist on multiple chains, in the same way as USDT. However, custodial Bitcoin may not be especially attractive and removes many of Bitcoin's key advantages.

The two largest and dominant stablecoins are USDT and USDC, both of which have a centralised custodian storing the underlying US Dollars in the banking system or treasury market. As mentioned earlier in this book, USDT is managed by Bitfinex. USDC, on the other hand, is run by a company called Circle. At the time of writing, there are US$68 billion and US$46 billion of USDT and USDC outstanding respectively. USDT has a much higher trading volume on the centralised exchanges, while USDC is more popular on smart contracts in Ethereum. USDT is therefore one of the most important tokens in the cryptocurrency space and USDT vs Bitcoin is the most liquid Bitcoin trading pair.

USDT

USDT originally launched as Realcoin in July 2014.[82] The coin was founded by Brock Pierce, a former Disney child actor and early cryptocurrency enthusiast. The coin was rebranded to US Dollar

---
[82] https://www.wsj.com/articles/BL-MBB-23780

Tether (USDT) in November 2014. USDT initially existed only on the Bitcoin blockchain, on a token layer called Omni. The Omni layer is a protocol which interprets extra meaning to otherwise surplus Bitcoin transaction data, for example the creation or transfer of USDT. From 2017 onwards, USDT was also available as a coin on the Ethereum blockchain and on the Litecoin blockchain. Due to the lower transaction fees on Ethereum at the time, USDT on Ethereum began to gain traction. Technically speaking, supporting USDT on Ethereum was the same work for wallets and exchanges as supporting the many other coins on Ethereum, because they used the same Ethereum token standard. For primarily this reason, Ethereum became the dominant venue for USDT, even as transaction fees increased. In contrast, USDT was the only major coin on Omni. More recently (from 2019), USDT also exists on the Tron network, another protocol competing with Ethereum.

USDT has not always performed perfectly with respect to the US Dollar peg. One of the main reasons for the deviations in price is uncertainty with respect to whether the coins are fully backed by US Dollars in the banking system or if there is a significant shortfall. Some examples of the most significant price deviations over history are provided below:

- **2016 Bitfinex hack** - As discussed earlier in this book, Bitfinex suffered a severe hack in August 2016. This caused the price of USDT to fall below US$1 for some periods.

- **2017 Bitfinex Wells Fargo lawsuit** - In April 2017, shortly after the shortfall relating to the 2016 hack had been dealt with, Bitfinex suffered delays with respect to US Dollar withdrawals and deposits. Bitfinex announced that "all incoming wires to Bitfinex will be blocked and refused by [the] Taiwan[ese] banks".[83] Bitfinex then filed a lawsuit against US bank Wells Fargo,[84] because the bank

---

[83] https://www.bitfinex.com/posts/200
[84] https://www.docdroid.net/jx1WRHX/bitfinex-vs-wells-fargo-pdf

"suspended US Dollar wire transfer operations needed to remit to [Bitfinex] customers". However, this lawsuit appeared to be a public relations move, designed to make customers realise the company was working hard to resolve these issues, actually winning the case seemed unlikely. At around the same time, a Twitter account called @Bitfinexed launched. This account, which now has over 83,000 followers, promoted the idea that USDT was not appropriately backed for years. At the time, Bitfinex was working very hard behind the scenes trying to establish and maintain banking relationships, something which was clearly very challenging, given the nature of USDT. With all this concern about solvency and banking partnerships, USDT traded at low at $0.91 in the period.

- **October 2018 solvency concerns** - Continued concerns surrounding the backing of USDT sent the price down to US$0.85 on the Kraken exchange in October 2018.[85] Temporary freezes of the USDT wallets of Binance and KuCoin worried some market participants.

- **April 2019 Crypto Capital Corp US$850 million loss** - On 25 April 2019 The New York Attorney General sued Bitfinex and published a series of documents.[86] The documents revealed that Bitfinex may have been using Tether's USDT reserves and appeared to lose US$850 million in loans to a Panamanian payment processing firm called Crypto Capital Corp. It was not clear who this counterparty was and Bitfinex claimed the funds were seized by a government, rather than being lost or stolen. Now it became clear that perhaps USDT did not have sufficient reserves and that Bitfinex may have put out misleading statements assuring customers that USDT was fully backed.

---

[85] https://newsaltcoins.com/crypto/tether-usdt-tremors-continue-as-dollar-peg-remains-far/

[86] https://iapps.courts.state.ny.us/fbem/DocumentDisplayServlet?documentId=vIexA1b0spKOnK_PLUS_ZUGTJ3A==&system=prod

Bitfinex went on to issue a new token, LEO,[87] to plug the hole.

- **May 2022 market contagion** - Finally, on 12 May 2022, USDT traded as low at US$0.948, as fear spread in the market about the solvency of various platforms.

It is critical to realise that not anyone can redeem and create USDT. In November 2017, Tether announced that creations and redemptions were no longer available to everyone on the official Tether website.

> We invite you to use the services of any one of a dozen global exchanges to acquire or dispose of Tethers for either USD or other cryptocurrencies. Such exchanges and other qualified corporate customers can contact Tether directly to arrange for creation and redemption.[88]

However, it is worth noting that even before November 2017, it is not clear if the creation and redemption process was available to the public. What changed from this point was that it became official, and only approved organisations could create and redeem USDT. The organisations are likely to have been cryptocurrency exchanges and large proprietary trading firms. It is also probably true that even within these approved organisations, they may not have all been in exactly the same position with regards to redemptions and creations. Some firms may have been able to redeem faster, due to their banking relationships or close relationships with Bitfinex or Tether. For example, if a trading firm has an account at the same bank at which the USDT reserves are held, the redemption process may be faster. Given the difficulty and challenges for Tether in establishing the right banking partners, Tether had an ever changing and complex web of banks all over the world. In 2018, a rumour was circulated which said Bitfinex had 14 staff whose full time job was opening bank accounts.

---

[87] https://www.bitfinex.com/wp-2019-05.pdf
[88] https://archive.ph/wpAUW

Some of the proprietary trading firms were playing a similar game, chasing Tether all over the world and constantly opening bank accounts. If they had a good relationship with Bitfinex and advanced notice, perhaps they could open new bank accounts with the same banks at the same time.

The implications of the failing US Dollar peg and the somewhat messy USDT redemption process are quite significant. It meant that when USDT traded at a discount, which as explained above happened quite often, those who could redeem USDT for US Dollars were often able to make extremely large profits in short periods of time. These funds could, for example, buy USDT for US$0.90 and redeem USDT for US$1. This trade could be repeated again and again. Therefore, it's possible that some organisations even had an incentive to spread rumours about the incomplete backing of USDT, to make handsome low risk profits. There is always the risk that USDT is actually insolvent and that holders could have a significant haircut, however if you were able to redeem quickly, perhaps in a day or two, the risk was minimal.

BitUSD

In addition to the centralised custodial stablecoins above, there is also the concept of a decentralised stablecoin, a crypto-token designed to follow the value of the US Dollar, without a centralised custodian. This is said to be one of the holy grails of financial technology. A stable US Dollar coin one can use online, without any counterparty risk and where transactions could never be blocked.

The first of these so-called decentralised stablecoins we will discuss is BitUSD, a stablecoin on the BitShares platform which launched in July 2014. BitShares was a delegated proof of stake (DPOS) platform launched in 2014 by Daniel Larimer, who went on to create the coin EOS several years later. This can be described as an algorithmic stablecoin, in that there were no US Dollars in the traditional banking system backing up the coin. One can argue that the coin was crypto-collateralised, in that there was a volatile cryptocurrency, BitShares, which one could redeem BitUSD for.

To create BitUSD, one needed to post BitShares as collateral. Initially there was a 150% maintenance margin, otherwise the BitUSD position could be liquidated. The price of BitShares vs BitUSD was determined on a decentralised exchange inside the BitShares system.

There did not appear to be a specific or strong price stability mechanism in the BitUSD system. One could redeem and create BitUSD, however the price this transfer occurred at was determined by the BitUSD vs BitShares price on a distributed exchange, which was not linked to "real" US Dollars. In a way the price references itself, it was therefore somewhat circular in logic. The argument put forward by some of the coins proponents was "Why would it trade at any other price?"

> *It implements automatic margin calls, such that if the price moves against someone who is effectively short, it forces them to cover and buy it back in the market and that creates a peg. The market peg works on the premise that all market participants buy and sell based on what they think market participants will be buying and selling in the future. The only rational choice is to assume that it's going to trade based on the peg in the future. If you don't believe that then you have to decide on which way it's going to go, up or down. And if you don't have a way of saying you abstain from the market. If you don't think it works you sell the shares and get out, as the system is going to fail in the first place. So its a self reinforcing market peg, that causes the asset to always have the purchasing power of the dollar. It's the same way dollars are created in the regular banking system. Dollars are lent into existence backed by collateral, in the case of the current banking*

> *system the collateral is your house. In the case of our system its shares in the DAC itself.*[89]

It should also be noted that BitUSD lacked a price oracle which could have linked the system to real world US Dollar price, one of the most controversial aspects of its design. However, any price oracle system is challenging to implement and may introduce several weaknesses and avenues for manipulation.

The volume of BitUSD in existence was a lot lower than many had hoped for, in some periods there was only around US$40,000 in issuance. At the same time liquidity was very low and the price stability was weak. The main architect of BitUSD went on to propose a new stablecoin called SteemUSD in 2017, this time including a price oracle system. While BitUSD was an interesting early experiment, it did not achieve what was hoped for.

In a way its design was naive and never could have scaled. With an algorithmic stablecoin, there is the possibility of turbulence in periods of volatile financial conditions. At the same time, sophisticated trading firms can try to short the stablecoin and end the peg, potentially producing significant profits.

DAI

The largest, most significant and most interesting algorithmic stablecoin is Dai, part of the Maker system on the Ethereum blockchain. This coin launched in December 2017. Its design was reasonably similar to BitUSD, except it had Ethereum as collateral and included external price feeds from price oracles. Again, there was a 150% minimum collateral requirement and holders of Dai could redeem for US$1 worth of Ethereum. These price feeds linked the real US Dollar vs Ethereum exchange rate to Dai. Maker is the governance token of the system and Maker coin holders can vote on policies with regards to the stabilisation mechanisms. While Dai had

---
[89] https://letstalkbitcoin.com/blog/post/lets-talk-bitcoin-129-dogeparty-and-delegated-proof-of-stake

many of the weaknesses of BitUSD, its design was far superior and the stability mechanism proved more effective. Today there are over US$6 billion of Dai in existence.

March 2020 Crash

In March 2020, financial markets were coming to terms with the level of disruption the policy response to COVID-19 was about to inflict on the global economy. As a result, asset prices started to rapidly decline in a crash. Bitcoin collapsed by around 50% to US$3,900. Ethereum experienced an even sharper decline, falling 64% to just US$90.

These sharp declines were exacerbated by cascading liquidations on the crypto-exchanges. The most significant of these was BitMEX, where a large number of traders with long positions were liquidated. The BitMEX trading engine then needed to close out these positions and took them over, as a result this drove the price down even further, causing more liquidations. Due to the size of these liquidation engine sell orders, the price of the perpetual swap contract on BitMEX traded well below the prevailing spot market price. On 12th March 2020, around US$753 million of long positions were liquidated on BitMEX.[90] On the perpetual swap contract Bitcoin reached a low of US$3,596, compared to a low of around US$3,915 in the spot market. This resulted in an attractive funding rate for those who went long the Bitcoin swap. The funding rate on BitMEX was 37.5 basis points for six eight hour periods in a row.[91] This equates to Bitcoin longs being offered around 410% per annum. However, in the market turmoil of the crash, traders were scrabbling for liquidity and were not attracted fast enough by this attractive rate, to close the price gap.

On 13th March 2020, BitMEX suffered two DDoS attacks,[92] ten hours apart and during these periods the trading engine was unable to

---

[90] https://decrypt.co/22172/bitcoin-flash-crash-liquidates-750-million-in-one-day
[91] https://www.bitmex.com/api/v1/funding?symbol=XBTUSD&columns=fundingRate&count=20&startTime=2020-03-12
[92] https://blog.bitmex.com/site_announcement/ddos-attack-13-march-2020/

execute significant orders and the Bitcoin price recovered.[93] At the time BitMEX thought it was a hardware issue. It is likely that the attacker discovered a vulnerability beforehand and then executed the attack when it would have the most significant market impact.[94] What may have actually caused the downtime was a bug in the customer chat system, the trollbox, which was exploited by sending it a query which clogged up all the computational resources of the server. This somehow prevented messages from being sent to the trading engine and caused the trading engine to fail.

In general, the OTC market and crypto-collateralised lending firms like BlockFi and Ledn appeared to handle the situation reasonably well. It was a rocky few days and many people were liquidated, but the liquidation processes appeared to function correctly. Many providers did not liquidate positions based on the spot price low of US$3,900 and allowed customer positions to remain open, waiting for the market to recover. BlockFi said the following:

> *We have continued to maintain perfect performance across all of our lending activities with zero losses in the lending book. Last Thursday (3/12) evening Eastern Time, there were particularly violent downward price movements in the cryptocurrency market resulting in very limited liquidity. This was handled strategically by our team and risk management system and we did not liquidate USD loan client collateral below a price of ~$4,500, despite the market reaching lows of ~$3,800. As a result of the team's prudent actions during this period, our clients' capital was saved and we also liquidated a smaller percentage (<10%) of our overall USD loan book vs. other market participants. Our system has processed the largest number and volume of daily deposits and withdrawals in BlockFi's history. Withdrawal*

---

[93] https://twitter.com/BitMEX/status/1238329954967752704
[94] https://blog.bitmex.com/how-we-are-responding-to-last-weeks-ddos-attacks/

processing is operating on our standard cycle and we remain ready to meet our clients' liquidity needs.[95]

In contrast to the OTC market players and lenders, Dai was not able to handle the sharp decline in the Ethereum price particularly smoothly. When the crash occurred, transaction volume on Ethereum spiked, causing severe network congestion. Part of the congestion was caused by liquidations of Dai positions. The feeds from the price oracles were also delayed by the network congestion.[96] The price of Dai was no longer stable. On 13th March 2020 Dai traded as high as US$1.12 and as low as US$0.96.[97]

As a result of this chaos, the Dai community realised that Ethereum was not suitable as the only form of collateral for Dai. If only Ethereum was used, it appeared inevitable that the stability system would eventually break. On 16th March 2020 there was a proposal to add USDC as a form of collateral.[98] This was adopted and from this point forwards a US Dollar backed custodial stablecoin was used as collateral for a so-called algorithmic stablecoin.

One can argue that using USDC to back Dai makes Dai pointless. Afterall, if the US authorities want to cease the USDC collateral they can, which will then result in the failure of Dai. However, there are some important differences. Dai now has all or nothing censorship, while USDC can be censored at will. USDC has a mechanism on Ethereum where individual accounts can be frozen and this has occurred several times,[99] typically at the request of law enforcement. However, Dai has no such individual account freeze feature. Instead, if law enforcement wants to freeze or censor anyone using Dai, they potentially must censor everyone, billions of dollars. It is possible we eventually reach the same end result, but in the short to medium term the dynamics are different.

---

[95] https://blockfi.com/an-update-on-blockfi-operations
[96] https://blog.makerdao.com/the-market-collapse-of-march-12-2020-how-it-impacted-makerdao/
[97] https://coinmarketcap.com/currencies/multi-collateral-dai/historical-data/
[98] https://blog.makerdao.com/executive-vote-usdc-march-16/
[99] https://www.coindesk.com/markets/2020/07/08/circle-confirms-freezing-100k-in-usdc-at-law-enforcements-request/

At the time of writing, there are US$6.4 billion Dai in existence and over 42% of the collateral is backed by the custodial stablecoin USDC. Only around 10% of the collateral is Ethereum. The collateral is also diversifying further, into traditional investment funds, even purchasing real estate. Part of the justification for this is that the Maker community are concerned that they are too dependent on USDC, which could at any point freeze all the balances at the request of US law enforcement. It is believed diversification will reduce this risk. A catalyst for this was the US Treasury's August 2022 decision to sanction the Ethereum mixer contract Tornado Cash.

UST

The final stablecoin we will discuss is UST, part of the Terra blockchain, which launched in April 2019. Like BitUSD years earlier, it can be considered an algorithmic stablecoin. There was a sister coin to UST, a proof of stake cryptocurrency called Luna. Luna was also the collateral backing up the stablecoin. If UST traded at a discount to the US Dollar, Luna tokens could be issued and UST holders should be able to, at least in theory, redeem their UST for US$1 worth of Luna. However, this mechanism has a clear and extremely obvious potential flaw. The new issuance of Luna could increase the supply of Luna in the market, which could cause the Luna price to decline. Then more and more Luna would need to be issued to maintain the peg, causing further price declines and a potential collapse of the system. However, for some reason, many seemed to overlook this and regarded UST as relatively safe.

The Terraform Labs company behind the chain was co-founded by Do Kwon and was incredibly successful in the 2021 period. By 2021, TerraForm Labs (TFL) was one of the VC darlings of the cryptocurrency space, regarded as having top technology and top marketing capabilities. In the company's most recent funding round in July 2021, Terraform Labs secured funding of over US$150 million, from investors such as Arrington Capital, BlockTower

Capital, Delphi Digital, Galaxy Digital, Hashed, Lightspeed Ventures and Pantera Capital.[100]

The UST stablecoin was a huge success in 2021 and early 2022. At the start of 2021 around US$180 million of UST were in issue and by the peak, in May 2022, the issuance reached over US$18 billion, with steady and consistent growth in the intervening period. The stability mechanism worked reasonably well. However, there were some periods where the algorithm did not achieve the desired stability and TFL had to intervene to maintain the peg. For instance, in December 2020, when the price of UST fell to US$0.85.[101]

It is certainly inaccurate to describe Mr Kwon as a modest individual. He is known for aggressively defending and promoting Luna and UST on Twitter. For example, when cryptocurrency analyst and fund manager Eric Wall criticised some of the mechanisms inside Luna, Mr Kwon Tweeted:

> *Reminder that unlike me, your rando ass blogs for a living. Do your job, or stay in irrelevance. That's all I ask.*[102]

In November 2021, another analyst provided a brief outline of how a wealthy attacker could break the UST system and profit, by conducting a "Soros style Black Wednesday attack". Mr Kwon responded by saying:

> *Probably the most retarded thread I've read this decade. Silence is a perfectly acceptable option if stupid. Billionaires in my following, go ahead, see what happens.*[103]

---

[100] https://archive.ph/beosy#selection-785.225-785.340
[101] https://coinmarketcap.com/currencies/terrausd/
[102] https://twitter.com/stablekwon/status/1508425097656549378
[103] https://twitter.com/stablekwon/status/1464897977793728514

Some of the arguments put forward by Do in defence of UST's stability systems, had echoes of the arguments put forward by Dan Larimer seven years earlier. Do compared UST to the way US Dollars are produced in the traditional banking system.

> *I do not think algorithmic stable coins fail because of algorithms, I think it fails because of the stability of the economies that are backing them. What I mean is an algorithmic stable coin and a national currency are actually very similar constructs. It is all based on the quantity theory of money. The idea is that you should be able to absorb contractions and expansions in currency and the best way to do that is to build a robust economy surrounding it.[104]*

Luna

UST's sister coin, Luna, was one of the best performing coins in the bull market of 2021. In January 2021 the coin was trading at around US$0.60. By the end of 2021 Luna traded at around US$90, amazing 15,000% returns. The coin continued to perform into 2022, reaching a peak price of around US$120 and a peak market capitalisation of over US$40 billion.

In September 2021, Do Kwon and TerraForm Labs (TFL) announced something called Project Dawn.[105] This was described as "a new funding initiative for critical infrastructure improvements and core technologies to supplement the accelerating growth of the Terra ecosystem". This essentially involved unlocking Luna tokens for use for TFL's operating expenses. The statement from Do Kwon read:

> *Project Dawn has commenced as of today with a 5 million LUNA unlocked and distributed by the TFL Genesis wallet (market value $150M). Further to*

---

[104] Do Kwon on the Laura Shin podcast
[105] https://medium.com/terra-money/introducing-project-dawn-5c2c8440c982

> *Project dawn, TFL is committing to unlock at most 3 million Luna per month for all operating costs with details around each unlock transparently relayed to the community.*

The spot price of Luna at the time was around US$30. This therefore implied TFL intended to spend US$90 million per month on operating expenditure, which is an exceptionally high budget. As for the details and transparency surrounding this, it's not clear such details were ever made available.

In February 2022, Terraform Labs announced a sponsorship deal with Major League Baseball's Washington Nationals, using US$40m of funds inside the Terra DAO. Luna holders had to vote inside the DAO to approve the sponsorship deal. The deal would mean the baseball team would sell tickets using UST.[106]

In January 2022, a foundation called the Luna Foundation Guard (LFG) was set up in Singapore.[107] Do Kwon was a founding member and director. The initial capital was a 50 million Luna gift from TFL. The LFG then began acquiring Bitcoin. On Twitter on 5 May 2022 the company stated:

> *The LFG has acquired an additional 37,863 Bitcoins totalling ~$1.5 billion in OTC swaps with @GenesisTrading and 3AC. The OTC swaps included 1 billion $UST for $1 billion worth of $BTC with Genesis, and the LFG purchased an additional $500 million worth of BTC via 3AC. The acquired BTC brings the LFG's total holdings to ~80,394 Bitcoins.[108]*

As a result of this the LFG had around US$3.5 billion of Bitcoin and the company announced that it planned to increase the holding to

---

[106] https://curlyw.mlblogs.com/nationals-terra-create-first-ever-sports-partnership-with-decentralized-autonomous-organization-20843cc704d3
[107] https://medium.com/terra-money/formation-of-the-luna-foundation-guard-lfg-6b8dcb5e127b
[108] https://mobile.twitter.com/LFG_org/status/1522234947070689280

US$10 billion. These funds were essentially obtained from the proceeds of the Luna coin offering and Luna coins allocated to TFL. The purpose of the Bitcoin holdings was to diversify the stability mechanism for UST. This could improve the robustness of UST, similar to how Dai diversified its collateral. Rather than only Luna backing up UST there could be a separate stability algorithm operating in parallel involving Bitcoin. Bitcoin is more liquid and stable than Luna, therefore this would reduce risk. In addition to this, with the Bitcoin backing UST, more Bitcoin would not be created if UST traded at a discount, instead reserves would be used and therefore there is no risk of a cascading collapse. Reserves were either sufficient or they were not. The idea was to construct a bridge between this custodial Bitcoin held by the LFG and the Luna blockchain, such that when inside Luna, the Bitcoin stability system could operate autonomously. These algorithmic stability systems involving Bitcoin were never constructed, nor was the bridge. Instead, the LFG just conducted manual interventions in the market using their reserves. The UST system never achieved an effective collateralisation level, unlike Dai for example, which was over collateralised. In addition to Bitcoin, the LFG also held an alternative coin called Avalanche (AVAX), for a similar reason but in a smaller quantity.

13

Defi

While the centralised cryptocurrency exchanges remained dominant in terms of volume and price formation, in 2020 decentralised exchanges started to gain traction. A centralised exchange means that the exchange is run by a single company on a server, alternatively, a decentralised exchange is when exchange processes, such as the execution of orders, matching and settlement occur on a distributed system, such as a blockchain. Critically, there is no custodial relationship between users and a decentralised exchange. A true distributed exchange (DEX), with an aggregated order book, should be considered as one of the other holy grails of financial technology. A truly unstoppable exchange could be transformational to the financial world.

The KYC Problem

A key problem for the centralised exchanges is regulatory pressure. Financial services are typically a highly regulated industry. Exchanges and derivatives markets in particular, are especially tightly regulated. The authorities and regulators may want to protect consumers from themselves, by limiting the types of products they can trade or invest in or restricting them from using certain platforms, especially unregulated platforms that could be hacked or lose client funds. For example, regulators could ban leverage over a certain threshold for retail customers, unless they jump through certain hoops. Another notable example is that the authorities may not want financial markets to cover certain areas like politics. In 2012 political betting platform Intrade was shut down by the US authorities (the

CFTC).[109] The authorities may also want to prevent or deter money laundering, forcing centralised exchanges to adopt know your customer (KYC) processes. Many users did not want to participate in the KYC process for a variety of reasons:

- The cumbersome KYC degraded the user experience of the platform.
- Users may refuse to participate in KYC for ideological privacy related reasons, perhaps as libertarian users, they do not believe the authorities should be able to see what financial activities they participate in.
- Users may be concerned about the platform storing their personal details and being hacked, a common occurrence in the space, which could jeopardise user privacy.
- Users may be trying to avoid capital gains tax on their cryptocurrency gains and do not want their respective governments to find out about their gains.
- Users could reside in a location where trading in the financial products they want to trade is banned.
- Users could actually be genuine money launderers, using cryptocurrency trading to hide the proceeds of crime.

While there are a variety of issues related to the KYC process, the truth is that the most significant was the degraded user experience of the cumbersome process, which often involved a photograph of the customer holding up an ID document, which was supposed to be visible to the camera. Retail traders want a fast and easy experience and easy access to leverage. KYC was therefore a major consideration in the marketplace. Platforms that avoided it or set higher thresholds before KYC applied, could gain market share.

This is where DeFi had an opportunity. If trading could be offered in a decentralised way using a blockchain, there would be no central entity the regulators could approach. This would be a dream for the libertarians and financial freedom advocates. Therefore, these

---

[109] https://www.cftc.gov/PressRoom/PressReleases/6423-12

decentralised platforms could offer a superior user experience and win in the market. Besides, a considerable part of the reasoning for regulations would no longer be applicable anyway, since a decentralised exchange was non-custodial, there was no risk of the exchange being hacked or otherwise running off with the money. On the other hand, it is possible a bug in the exchange's smart contract could result in an equivalent loss for customers.

Decentralised Exchanges

A DEX is certainly technically possible, within the confines of a single blockchain ecosystem and the tokens which exist within that system. Since all the tokens are native to the blockchain, one can build an exchange, with a centralised order book and clearing mechanism on top of the blockchain. This can be done on Ethereum for example. The main challenges are scalability, liquidity, usability and ensuring the fairness of the exchange.

Counterparty

Back in 2013, what is widely regarded as the first Initial Coin Offering (ICO) in the space occurred, Mastercoin. The aim of the project was to be a protocol to launch multiple tokens on top of Bitcoin. Essentially surplus Bitcoin transaction data was interpreted by the Mastercoin protocol, as issuing or spending additional tokens. A Mastercoin foundation was set up to manage the proceeds from the ICO. However, there was considerable pushback from the community about the foundation and the unfairness behind the idea that a select few would be given the privilege of managing and controlling the ICO funds.

Therefore, towards the start of 2014, a rival project was set up, Counterparty. This had the same premise as Mastercoin and also had a token, XCP, compared to Mastercoin's MSC. However, rather than having an ICO, where a select group would manage the funds, there was a "proof of burn", where Bitcoin were sent to a provably unspendable address and the initial XCP coin allocation was decided by who destroyed the most Bitcoin. This avoided the need for a controversial foundation. Due perhaps to this "fairer" token launch, and the hard work of lead developer Adam Krellenstein, the Counterparty protocol succeeded in becoming the dominant token issuance platform in the space. The XCP token itself was necessary to pay a fee to create new tokens, however other than that there was limited use for it.

The most interesting and exciting feature of Counterparty was undoubtedly the DEX. All Counterparty tokens could be traded on the DEX, which operated on top of the Bitcoin network. A Bitcoin transaction had extra data which could be interpreted by the Counterparty protocol as either a bid, an offer or an order cancellation. If a Bitcoin block contained a matching bid and offer, the protocol would consider the trade executed.

Counterparty's DEX failed to gain significant traction, primarily for five reasons:

- **User experience** – The user experience was not compelling, particularly due to Bitcoin's target block time interval of ten minutes, which normally means users had to wait several minutes after taking an action, like submitting an order, before it appeared on the order book.

- **Lack of liquidity** – Liquidity on the DEX was low and there was little incentive to be a market maker. At the same time adjusting orders was a time consuming and difficult process, which resulted in market makers having to conduct cumbersome and high risk on-chain processes, to maintain liquid markets with tight spreads. Market makers were also exposed to the risks of miners front running their orders. Liquidity essentially dried up on the platform for most of the time.

- **Scalability** – Bitcoin fees were already becoming significant at this point, especially for large Counterparty transactions. Having to pay a large fee, perhaps a dollar, just to submit an order, was too much of a burden for some.

- **Perceived Bitcoin culture** – Perhaps even more important than scalability was the cultural issue. Some in the Bitcoin community did not welcome this kind of activity on-chain. They considered Bitcoin as more serious than all these "joke tokens". Many considered that the DEX would increase validation costs, increase transaction fees or result in misaligned incentives. It is this cultural perception that drove much of the token issuance and DEX type activity away from Bitcoin.

- **Timing** – The ecosystem was simply too small and niche at the time to be ready for DEXs. Many members of the community were still familiarising themselves with more basic concepts such as transaction confirmations.

Mastercoin eventually rebranded as Omni and the old Mastercoin token was no longer used. USDT was then issued on the Omni layer and this eventually became a large success, as Counterparty faded into irrelevance. Later on, USDT migrated to other chains and even Omni was barely used.

IDEX

The Counterparty model was emulated, to some extent, on Ethereum by the first generation of Ethereum DEXs in around 2018. Since most of the alternative tokens, by value, exist on Ethereum rather than Bitcoin, developers have little choice but to select Ethereum as their DEX platform. As there was now a rich and wide variety of tokens that existed on Ethereum due to the 2017 ICO boom. These DEXs were therefore more attractive to speculators. The most notable and popular of these Ethereum DEXs in 2018 was IDEX.

Like Counterparty four years earlier, on IDEX, bids, offers and order cancellations were submitted to the Ethereum blockchain, resulting in one aggregated order book. Traders deposited funds into an Ethereum smart contract and the signature of both the traders and the IDEX platform was required to submit orders, execute trades, or make payments.

However, to solve many of the user experience issues, orders were centrally submitted to an IDEX server first, after which IDEX then added their signature to the transaction before broadcasting it to the Ethereum network. Order submission, order cancellation, and order matching was conducted off-chain on the IDEX servers, to allow for a fast and seamless user experience. The events were then submitted in sequence to the Ethereum blockchain and are only valid with a valid signature from the users. After a certain time horizon, users could withdraw funds from the smart contract without a signature from IDEX, which protects user deposits in the event that IDEX disappears. Therefore, IDEX was unable to steal user funds or conduct trades without user authorisation. On the other hand, users had to trust a central entity to determine the sequence of events, but the exchange is still non-custodial. This was essentially a non-custodial exchange rather than a true DEX. However, this was still an interesting achievement and business model.

In early 2019, IDEX was the global number one Ethereum-based DEX, with an approximate market share of 50%. Trading volume was around US$1 million per day at the peak. IDEX failed to generate significant market traction, the primary problem was the difficulty in generating liquidity, due in part to the large amount of on-chain data which would be generated by would be market makers. The model did not work for a blockchain with the capacity of Ethereum.

Uniswap & Curve

The next group of DEX protocols to cover is Uniswap, and another similar project, Curve. Uniswap launched towards the end of 2018, the protocol enjoyed slow and steady growth until 2020, when growth skyrocketed. After years of trial and error, this is finally a model that is a success story, with significant trading volume. Rather than having the traditional order book structure, Uniswap and Curve use liquidity pools for each trading pair. The concept of these reserve liquidity pools is said to originate from the Bancor protocol, first described in a 2017 paper.[110] Those who participate in these pools provide liquidity for traders, with different liquidity pools for each trading pair. These liquidity providers are often called automated market markets (AMM), in contrast to the traditional non automated "manual" market makers on centralised platforms. And yes, you guessed it, by participating in these pools one can earn a yield.

This is a bit of an oversimplification, but the price ratio between two tokens can basically be calculated by dividing the numbers of each token locked in the liquidity pool. For example, take the USDC vs Ethereum trading pair. If the pool contains 4,000 USDC and 10 Ethereum, the Ethereum price can be calculated as 4,000/10 = US$400. This means that each side of the pool has around the same value in it. In simple terms, this US$400 price is the value at which the smart contract allows one to trade Ethereum for USDC or USDC for Ethereum, at least in small amounts. USDC vs Ethereum tended to be the most popular trading pair in DeFi.

This ingenious but reasonably simple mechanism incentivises liquidity providers to ensure the value of the two tokens in the liquidity pool is at the appropriate level. If the market price of one of the tokens changes and market makers do not adjust the liquidity pool sizes, traders could exploit this by purchasing tokens at a lower than market price. Going back to our earlier example, if the price of Ethereum suddenly crashes to US$200, traders would be incentivised to use the smart contract to sell Ethereum to the pool, thereby adding Ethereum to the pool and removing USDC. The losses liquidity

---

[110] https://whitepaper.io/document/52/bancor-whitepaper

providers suffer as a result of these price movements is known as impermanent loss.

The above methodology works to some extent, however it still needs to address the issue of liquidity, slippage and large orders. The core operating principle behind Uniswap, created to address this liquidity issue, is related to the curve $y = 1/x$. The x and y-axis represent the number of tokens of each coin in the liquidity pool and each point on the curve represents a possible state of the pools. The liquidity pools will only accept and execute a trade if the area under the new equilibrium point is higher than the area before the swap. This means that if a trader submits a larger order, they will execute at an inferior price to a trader with a smaller order. In general, the higher the volume one wishes to trade, the more slippage the trader will experience.

The Curve protocol can have a unique equation for each trading pair, which can be set according to the market structure of the coins in question, depending on for example the expected price volatility between the two coins. Hence the name Curve.

With this AMM system there is no orderbook, but merely two pools of funds and this alone is sufficient for trading. This makes market making far easier than constantly using the blockchain to adjust orders, as blockchains may not have the capacity for this. In normal market conditions, market makers can just provide liquidity into the pool instead of regularly adjusting their orders as the price changes, significantly reducing the usage of the cumbersome and expensive blockchain. This clever mechanism essentially partly solved the liquidity and scalability problems with respect to Counterparty and IDEX.

When providing this liquidity on Uniswap or Curve, you can earn a yield. For example, when a trade is executed on Uniswap, a fee of 0.3% is charged. These fees are then sent to the liquidity providers, in proportion to the amount of liquidity which has been provided.

Trading activity on these DEXs rapidly picked up in the summer of 2020, the so-called summer of DeFi. According to CoinGecko, in February 2020 less than US$1 billion of volume occurred on these protocols. By August 2020 monthly trading volume had reached US$12.7 billion. In 2021 the market picked up further. In May 2021 monthly trading volume peaked at over US$200 billion. Uniswap accounted for almost 60% of the volume of these DEX's in most months. In contrast, Curve was doing around 10% of DEX market volume. In 2021, total DeFi trading volume represented around 8% to 9% of the spot volume on centralised cryptocurrency exchanges. This is a remarkable success, especially since much of the centralised cryptocurrency exchange volume has very low fees and therefore volume can be cheaply manipulated. In the first half of 2022, DeFi trading volumes were around the same as 2021, however the market share compared to centralised exchanges grew substantially, as centralised exchange volume declined in 2022 after the 2021 bull market. DeFi trading volume had proved more robust than the centralised competition, quite a success story.

With trading volume on the DeFi protocols skyrocketing in 2021, liquidity providers were earning excellent returns. By placing your USDC in a Uniswap liquidity pool in 2020 and 2021, one could often earn between 15% and 40%. Institutional money was of course slow to deploy to this new area and therefore many specialist cryptocurrency trading firms who were quick to adapt to this performed extremely well. Alameda Research, owned by Sam Bankman-Fried (SBF), who also founded the cryptocurrency trading platform FTX, is perhaps the best example of this.

Food Tokens

It is worth remembering what is driving everything in the space, a desire to speculate on tokens. The narratives were first created by the Bitcoiners. Dreamy narratives about advanced disruptive technology, banking the unbanked, disintermediation, fixing a broken economic system dependent on ever expanding debt and of tokens going to the moon. These narratives were then copied, manipulated, refined and adapted for a growing range of coins, coins which were getting more and more outrageous as time progressed.

Merely trading speculative coins on a DEX and earning decent yields for providing liquidity to facilitate these trades was not enough for some people. Instead, the DeFi contracts enabling this trade and yield could also have their own native tokens. These tokens could be awarded to liquidity providers, a reward for providing liquidity. These newly issued token rewards could then supplement the yield. Liquidity providers could then have two sources of income, trading fees and newly issued token rewards. Traders could also be awarded these newly issued tokens as a reward for trading on the DEX platforms. These new tokens could also appreciate in value, a virtuous cycle creating more and more wealth and more and more yield. With this token issuance model, yields could be a lot higher than 15% to 40%. One could earn 40% or 80%. When a protocol was new, the advertised yields could be even higher, in the thousands or even millions of percent per annum. Of course, these rates were extremely volatile and not sustainable for any reasonable amount of time.

For some reason, many of these DEX contracts were named after food. For example, SushiSwap and PancakeSwap being two of the most famous. There was also Burger Swap, Yam Finance, Bakery Swap, Pizza, Hotdog Swap and Kimchi Finance, just to give a few examples. The more obscure, new and mad the platform was, the higher the yield one could earn from it. In some cases it was less and less clear what the smart contract and token actually did. One could just deposit funds into a smart contract and earn a ludicrously high yield, based on the new tokens being issued. The annual yield was sometimes quoted in so many digits, it wasn't easy to determine how large it was. Was the annual yield in the billions or trillions of percent? If it even mattered. It was almost as if the more stupid a token was, the more yield needed to be offered to attract investors.

In an infamous interview with Bloomberg in April 2022, Sam Bankman-Fried (SBF) controversially, but somewhat accurately described the situation as follows:

> *Let me give you sort of like a really toy model of it, which I actually think has a surprising amount of legitimacy for what farming could mean. You know, where do you start? You start with a company that builds a box and in practice this box, they probably dress it up to look like a life-changing, you know, world-altering protocol that's gonna replace all the big banks in 38 days or whatever. Maybe for now actually ignore what it does or pretend it does literally nothing. It's just a box. So what this protocol is, it's called 'Protocol X,' it's a box, and you take a token. You can take Ethereum, you can put it in the box and you take it out of the box. Alright so, you put it into the box and you get like, you know, an IOU for having put it in the box and then you can redeem that IOU back out for the token.*
>
> *So far what we've described is the world's dumbest ETF or ADR or something like that. It doesn't do anything but let you put things in it if you so choose. And then this protocol issues a token, we'll call it whatever, 'X token.' And X token promises that anything cool that happens because of this box is going to ultimately be usable by, you know, governance vote of holders of the X tokens. They can vote on what to do with any proceeds or other cool things that happen from this box. And of course, so far, we haven't exactly given a compelling reason for why there ever would be any proceeds from this box, but I don't know, you know, maybe there will be, so that's sort of where you start.*

And then you say, alright, well, you've got this box and you've got X token and the box protocol declares, or maybe votes by on-chain governance, or, you know, something like that, that what they're gonna do is they are going to take half of all the X tokens that were re-minted. Maybe two thirds will, two thirds will offer X tokens, and they're going to give them away for free to whoever uses the box. So anyone who goes, takes some money, puts in the box, each day they're gonna airdrop, you know, 1% of the X token pro rata amongst everyone who's put money in the box. That's for now, what X token does, it gets given away to the box people. And now what happens? Well, X token has some market cap, right? It's probably not zero. Let say it's, you know, a $20 million market

You might think, for instance, that in like five minutes with an internet connection, you could create such a box and such a token, and that it should reflect like, you know, it should be worth like $180 or something market cap for like that, you know, that effort that you put into it. In the world that we're in, if you do this, everyone's gonna be like, 'Ooh, box token. Maybe it's cool. If you buy in box token,' you know, that's gonna appear on Twitter and it'll have a $20 million market cap. And of course, one thing that you could do is you could like make the float very low and whatever, you know, maybe there haven't been $20 million dollars that have flowed into it yet. Maybe that's sort of like, is it, you know, mark to market fully diluted valuation or something, but I acknowledge that it's not totally clear that this thing should have market cap, but empirically I claim it would have market cap.[111]

---

[111] https://www.bloomberg.com/news/articles/2022-04-25/odd-lots-full-transcript-sam-bankman-fried-and-matt-levine-on-crypto

Leverage

Systems like Uniswap and Curve can almost be considered as a base layer of DeFi. It was akin to the centralised spot exchanges. All you could do with them is swap tokens and provide liquidity. What traders really wanted was leverage. DeFi also provided this. Ethereum smart contracts such as Compound & AAVE allowed users to deposit a coin as collateral, to borrow another coin. What made these systems so popular was the ability to combine borrowing with DEXs, to increase leverage and speculate on price changes. Just like the borrowing on Bitfinex around seven years earlier, people were not borrowing to invest in the real economy, they were borrowing to speculate on cryptocurrency tokens with leverage.

For example, one could provide Ethereum as collateral on Compound and borrow Dai. Then, in a second step, use Uniswap to swap this Dai back into Ethereum. Then, step three would be to use the Ethereum as collateral Compound again, borrowing more Dai. This cycle of rehypothecation can occur multiple times. Thereby, using multiple DeFi protocols to obtain leverage to increase exposure to Ethereum. This is just what some of the Ledn clients were doing in the centralised world. Now they could do this on DeFi too, with zero KYC. In order to borrow, typically there is a collateral requirement of around 75%, which means if you have US$100 worth of Ethereum in your account, you could borrow up to US$75 worth of Dai or USDC. If an account falls below the necessary collateral requirement, the smart contract liquidates the position. The way this works is that other users can repay a portion of the debt and in return receive a portion of the collateral. The account who took over the liquidated position purchases the collateral at a discount, for example an 8% discount, which encourages them to take over the position. The smart contract calculates the solvency of each account by using third party price oracles, who submit price data into the Ethereum blockchain.

Both Compound and AAVE were relatively similar in terms of scale. In the summer of 2020, both platforms had a few million dollars in outstanding debt. From this point onwards debt levels expanded rapidly, each growing to around US$8 billion of debt by around May 2021. The most common coins that were borrowed were Dai and USDC, which dominated the outstanding debt.

The rate at which you could borrow the US Dollar stablecoins on Compound was quite volatile. The variable interest rate typically ranged from between 5% to 20% from the summer of 2020 until the end of 2021. During periods of peak cryptocurrency speculation, for example, in April 2021, rates were at elevated levels, typically at around 13%, based on seven day moving averages. These attractive rates were much higher than the official base rate in the economy, which was near zero at the time. When investors were starved of yield, deploying capital into DeFi and engaging in reasonably low risk lending, due to strong collateral requirements, was quite attractive.

Somewhat ironically, as the cryptocurrency bull market ended, towards the end of 2022 the DeFi borrow rate declined to around 2%, lower than the base rate set by the Federal Reserve. Lending US Dollars in DeFi in the second half of 2022 was far less attractive. In contrast the rate at which one could borrow Ethereum on Compound has always been stable and low. Ranging from about 2% to 3%. One could also borrow Bitcoin on Compound, custodial Bitcoin in the form of WBTC, a service provided by a company called Bitgo. Here rates were typically lower than US Dollar stablecoin rates, but far more volatile than Ethereum rates. The Bitcoin borrow rate was typically around 4%, with the occasional spike up towards 10% or even 20% at times. The cost to borrow all the other cryptocurrencies was almost always higher than Ethereum, although volume here was much lower.

Compound - USDC Lending Rates (Weekly Averages)

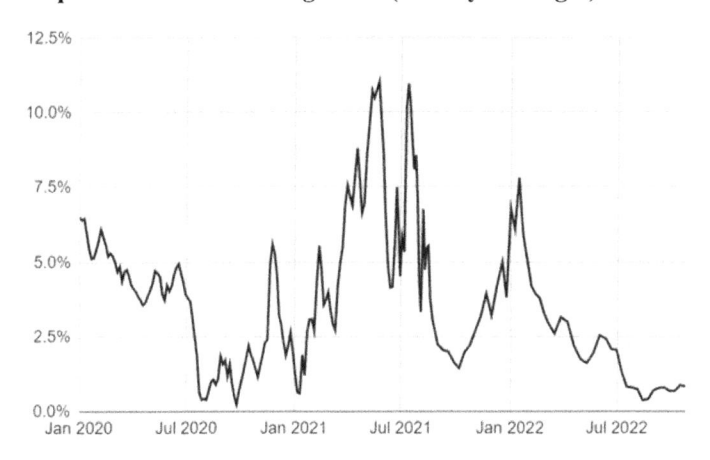

Source: The Block

May 2021 Crash

May 2021 saw a cryptocurrency price crash. From 15 May 2021 to 19 May 2021 the Ethereum price crashed by 53%, from over US$4,000 to under US$2,000. The Bitcoin price also declined from about US$56,000 to US$38,000 in the period. In the grand scheme of things this was not a big deal. Indeed, the Ethereum price had been at the US$2,000 level just a month earlier. Of course, cryptocurrency had crashed significantly before, for example March 2020, which was covered earlier in this book. The reason this crash was potentially significant, was because it was the first major correction since DeFi had taken off.

Some of the critics of DeFi had made the following argument:
- DeFi systems are used to speculate on tokens and there are very few other legitimate use cases of DeFi.
- There is considerable debt and leverage in the DeFi system, at unsustainably high levels. This leverage is the epicentre and critically the fundamental cause of the extreme cryptocurrency price appreciation experienced in 2021.

Ethereum is considered a high-powered machine of speculation and leverage.
- Much of the capital has entered DeFi due to dangerously high yields on offer, which are not sustainable.
- The DeFi boom has occurred in a bull market and in that environment it works fine. However, when times change and a crash happens, we will see cascading liquidations across DeFi.
- The smart contracts may struggle to handle the extent of liquidations, perhaps due to bugs and the Ethereum network will become congested.
- The large amount of deleveraging may prove that most DeFi protocols are economically weak and susceptible to attacks.
- The value of funds locked inside the protocols will decline rapidly and many users will lose funds and the system will struggle to recover.
- The price of many cryptocurrencies will then crash and we will enter a prolonged bear market cycle.

There are of course many truths to these criticisms, which were articulated by some sophisticated macro investors in the period. However, by and large, the DeFi protocols handled the crash reasonably well and the critics were shown to be mostly wrong. In May 2021 there were US$400 million and US$300 million of liquidations on AAVE and Compound respectively. The most common form of collateral which was liquidated was Ethereum, followed by WBTC, which were both used to borrow US Dollar stablecoins. AAVE witnessed small drawdowns in the outstanding loan balance, before quickly continuing with its upwards trajectory. The centralised cryptocurrency exchanges processed around US$10 billion of long liquidations during the May 2021 crash.[112]

As for Ethereum network congestion, the lending protocols handled this reasonably well, at least much better than some protocols handled the March 2020 crash. Ethereum fees did spike much more in 2021

---

[112] https://medium.com/gauntlet-networks/aave-protocol-liquidation-retrospective-may-2021-67c655fc1b31

than in 2020, the top paying transactions paid around ten times more in the May 2021 crash than the March 2020 crash. However, the key liquidation orders did get through into the blockchain in a timely manner. Around US$35 million of positions were liquidated because the loan repayment transactions were not processed by the network in time, as the transaction fees were too low. This is not great for the traders involved, but this is a far lower value than it could have been.

Critics of DeFi could still argue that the crash was not large enough to cause the pain and chaos some had anticipated. It could also be argued that some of the most successful and highly profitable trading shops with large balance sheets had provided liquidity, in a coordinated way, at critical times during the May 2021 crash to prevent widespread cascading DeFi liquidations.

While it may have been true that 2021 can be characterised as an outrageous, unsustainable, leveraged and greed driven cryptocurrency bubble, it's probably not true to say that DeFi caused the bubble, nor is it true to say DeFi was at the bubble's epicentre. The lesson from the May 2021 crash was that the mechanics and structure of the market was somewhat different than the DeFi critics had expected. The leading DeFi protocols were more resilient than the critics thought. It was centralised actors which were to blame for the most severe extremities of the 2021 bubble. However, of course within DeFi there were examples of sheer madness, such as the food tokens. But the most egregious and stupid lending decisions appeared to have been made using traditional centralised systems, rather than on DeFi.

The Anchor Protocol

One of the key drivers in the growth of Luna and the UST stablecoin was a lending system called the Anchor protocol. This newer system may not have had the resilience of protocols like AAVE and Compound. Anchor was a lending protocol on the Luna blockchain, where users could make deposits into the system and earn a yield.

Anchor deposits climbed from around US$50 million in March 2021 to an astonishing peak of around US$15 billion at the end of April 2022. This deposit balance experienced solid straight line type growth throughout the period, just like the UST outstanding balance growth.

Typically, around 40% to 60% of UST in issuance was deployed in the Anchor protocol. A fraction of these deposits was lent out. At the peak, the loan book was around US$3.5 billion, a loan to value ratio of around 30% compared to the deposit base. The Anchor protocol also had a governance token called ANC.

The Anchor protocol was all about yield, paying depositors an attractive and stable yield of 20%. This 20% rate was key to the marketing behind Anchor and indeed UST. The objective of the protocol was to stabilise interest rates, compared to the more volatile rates on the other DeFi lending protocols in Ethereum.

The protocols on Ethereum, such as AAVE and Compound, connect lenders and borrowers together. Anchor works slightly differently, instead of more directly connecting borrowers and lenders, there is a pool of reserves in the protocol in the middle, called the yield reserve. Borrowers borrow from the reserve fund, making interest payments to the reserve fund. On the other hand, depositors send funds into the reserve and receive interest payments from the reserve fund. The interest rates are claimed to be algorithmically determined, by a formula that uses the size of the various pools of funds. The core advantage of this structure, compared to AAVE and Compound, was that interest rates were more stable as the reserve fund could weather the impact of short-term imbalances in supply and demand. The system was described in the Anchor whitepaper as follows.

> *The core building block of the Anchor savings protocol is the Terra money market – a WASM (Web Assembly) smart contract on the Terra blockchain that facilitates depositing and borrowing of Terra stablecoins (TerraUSD, for instance). The money market is defined*

by a pool of Terra deposits that earns interest from borrowers. Borrowers put down digital assets as collateral to borrow Terra from the pool. The interest rate is determined algorithmically as a function of borrowing demand and supply, which is encoded by the pool's [utilisation] ratio (fraction of Terra in the pool that has been borrowed).[113]

This book does not attempt to cover the formula for determining these interest rates in detail and it does not appear that this formula was actually used. Instead, the interest rates seemed to be controlled by TFL.

Throughout the existence of Anchor, because only around 30% of the funds deposited were loaned out, due to a lack of demand to borrow, the protocol had negative cash flows. This means that interest payments were higher than interest receipts. The yield reserve fund was therefore continually drained.

In October 2021 the yield reserve was around US$70 million, due to the initial capital it was provided with by TFL. By February 2022 this had been depleted to just US$6 million.[114] At this point Do Kwon announced via Twitter that the LFG would inject 450 million UST into the yield reserve fund.[115] Without this injection of capital, the fund could not afford the interest payments. The 20% yield could therefore be maintained and the yield reserve fund continued to be depleted into the first half of 2022. As yields in DeFi continued to decline into 2022, the promised 20% yield became less and less sustainable. Therefore, rather than the algorithmically determined interest rates which the whitepaper proposed, it appeared as if the TFL was determining the interest rates manually, by artificially injecting capital into the reserve fund to maintain the 20% rate.

---

[113] https://www.anchorprotocol.com/docs/anchor-v1.1.pdf
[114] https://www.theblock.co/data/decentralized-finance/cryptocurrency-lending/anchor-yield-reserve
[115] https://twitter.com/stablekwon/status/1494470634042060800

The decision to keep the deposit rate at 20% was controversial at the time and many saw the yield as unsustainable. In early 2022 venture firm Polychain Capital argued yield paid outs on balances exceeding 100,000 UST should be reduced. A formal governance proposal was created, which would see deposits under 100,000 UST receive 19.56%, while deposits between 100,000 UST and 500,000 UST would be paid 17.5% and deposits valued greater than 500,000 UST would get 10%. The proposal suggested reducing the rates for medium and large deposits linearly over 19 months at 30-day increments. Caps like this would keep the small retail depositors happy, while lowering rates for larger investors and adopt a similar cap system structure to centralised lending platforms like BlockFi. However, the proposal lost the vote, with over three-quarters of the votes rejecting it.[116] The aim of the proposal was to make the Anchor protocol more sustainable and keep interest rates more realistic, given the prevailing market conditions of declining returns across the DeFi space.

Continuing to subsidise the yield, with money from the LFG could not last forever. Remember, the LFG funds were raised from outside investors (directly or indirectly via Luna sales) and eventually the investor funds would run out and the system would be dependent on more and more investors to keep it running. It is also not clear if investing in a company to subsidise returns for other investors, is an intelligent investment strategy. On the other hand, in this case, many of the initial investors in Luna, TFL and the LFG, may have been the same entities which were participating in Anchor.

The proposal was probably rejected for several reasons. It is possible many of the voters were receiving these 20% interest payments and wanted these good times to continue. In particular, many of the entity's earning interest may have borrowed money at perhaps around 10% and were making a killing on the 10% spread. They wanted these good times to continue.

---

[116] https://thedefiant.io/terra-anchor-proposal-yield-rejected

The announcement of the 450 million UST capital injection sent the price of Luna skyrocketing, up from US$50 to US$90 in a few days. This represented significant outperformance compared to other cryptocurrencies such as Ethereum. It is likely that Do Kwon and other Luna investors wanted to keep the party going.

Just like BlockFi, the philosophy of Luna and Anchor was about winning users and growth. It was fine if the Anchor reserve was depleted over the short to medium term, because it was about winning market share and attracting users. Over the long term, once Anchor was the winner, it could lower the deposit rate and start to sustainably generate cash flow. The 450 million UST spend was considered as a marketing cost for TFL. At the time, many considered Anchor as the largest DeFi protocol in the world, with the amount deposited exceeding any other DeFi project on Ethereum. Anchor was working and it was winning, while cryptocurrency, blockchain, DeFi and web3 was a major global paradigm shift. TFL/LFG had significant reserves, due to the skyrocketing Luna price and it was certainly worth spending the cash in the short term to secure Anchor's position as the winner. At least this is what they are likely to have thought at the time.

Back Down To Earth

Anchor aside, which perhaps wasn't really a DeFi project after all, DeFi involves highly complex and advanced technological innovations. These technologies can enable people to engage in new types of financial activity, which could transform the world of finance. On the other hand, it's still appropriate to be sceptical about DeFi. DeFi needs to be evaluated in the right context. DeFi is used by traders wishing to speculate on cryptocurrency prices, often with leverage. DeFi is very much a continuation or replacement of what happened on Bitfinex in 2016 and then BitMEX in 2018. As a platform for this kind of trading, DeFi is successful and some of the larger, more established and stronger DeFi platforms, like Uniswap and AAVE are reasonably robust. However, hopes of DeFi based systems revolutionising finance in the real economy, for example helping provide finance for real world investment projects in a meaningful way, are somewhat farfetched, at least at this point.

In 2021 one could earn attractive yields on DeFi and doing so appeared exciting, it seemed the way of the future. Many people wanted to deploy capital into DeFi, however it was more challenging than many people expected. Managing liquidity pools and being in the loop about the next new high yield token was too challenging for many potential investors. This is where the earn business model comes in. One could deposit cryptocurrency with the earn platforms and they could deploy this money into DeFi for you. Alternatively, the earn platform could lend your funds out to specialist proprietary trading firms, who could deploy the money into DeFi. The investors would therefore never need to worry about impermanent loss, managing private keys, dealing with skyrocketing Ethereum gas fees or dealing with various front running type DeFi attacks, but they could still earn the amazing returns DeFi offered. DeFi could be accessed via intermediaries and some of the earn platforms had a nice and friendly narrative explaining the attractive yields they provided, it was DeFi.

14

Crypto Credit Market Structure

Grayscale

Grayscale is a leading cryptocurrency asset management platform and part of Barry Silbert's Digital Currency Group (DCG). In October 2015 Sibert announced that DCG raised money, with funding from Bain Capital Ventures, Transamerica Ventures, FirstMark Capital, MasterCard, and New York Life.[117] Silbert first rose to fame in the Bitcoin space in 2014, for winning an auction to purchase Bitcoins confiscated from the darknet market the Silk Road, which was conducted by the US Marshals Service.

Grayscale provides US listed cryptocurrency exchange traded products (ETPs), in the form of trusts. The group's main product was the Grayscale Bitcoin Trust (GBTC). This product was extremely successful, attracting considerable inflows from investors. As the following chart indicates, the product achieved a market capitalisation of almost US$40 billion in 2021.

The product was expensive, it had a large 2% annual management fee on the net asset value. Grayscale's business was therefore extremely cash generative. For example, if the average GBTC net asset value in a year was US$10 billion, this could generate US$200 million in very high profit margin revenues for Grayscale. Grayscale and DCG therefore quickly emerged as one of the key financial powerhouses within the industry. The company is likely to have had a very strong

---

[117] https://techcrunch.com/2015/10/27/barry-silbert-launches-digital-currency-group-with-funding-from-mastercard-others/#!

balance sheet and therefore the group was one of the counterparties others could trust and depend on.

GBTC Market Capitalisation - US$ Billions

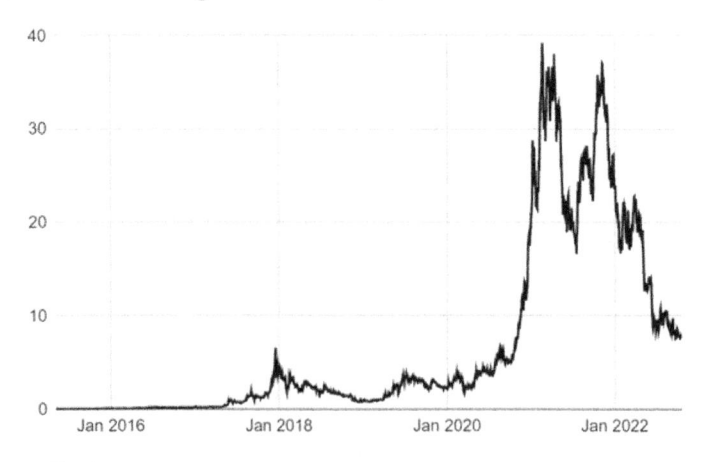

Source: Bloomberg

GBTC was an extremely poor product from the point of view of investors. The key weakness is that it was a trust and the Bitcoin backing the fund could not be redeemed. This means that the fund can continue to accumulate Bitcoin reserves and its reserves can never decline. One would think that with a structure like this, the trust would trade at a steep discount to the underlying asset, however as the following chart shows, for most of its life, the trust traded on a large premium to the underlying Bitcoin.

GBTC Premium/Discount to the Net Asset Value

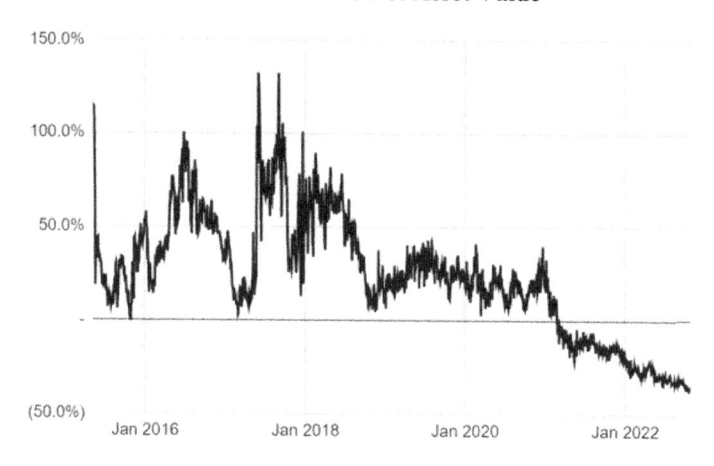

Source: Bloomberg

As the above chart illustrates, the tracking performance of GBTC has been outrageously poor. The premium has on occasions been over 100% and for years at a time the premium has sustained at a level over 30%. More recently, the trust has been trading at a steep discount to the value of the underlying Bitcoin in the trust.

Given the lack of a redemption mechanism, explaining the premium can be challenging. The theory is that investors purchase the trust on the market, because there are limited options available when trying to obtain Bitcoin exposure in one's normal brokerage account. It is this lack of competition, particularly in the US market, which may have driven up the premium. Purchasing a traditional trust is far easier than buying real Bitcoin for most investors, given the challenges involved in managing private keys. In particular, institutional investors who are required to comply with various regulations may be unable to purchase Bitcoin directly, while they may be keen on exposure due to Bitcoin's rapid price appreciation and success in the period. Therefore, some investors were willing to purchase the trust at a large premium. It is also possible some investors were poorly informed and did not know the vehicle was trading at such a large premium, these non-sophisticated investors may have just wanted Bitcoin exposure.

One may ask why arbitrageurs cannot simply profit from this and narrow the spread. Some accredited investors can create new units of the fund at the net asset value, however the process of creating new units can take up to six months. Therefore, although some trading firms were conducting arbitrage and closing the gap, clearly most of the time the trust still traded at a large premium as the arbitrageurs could not keep up with the demand for Bitcoin.

The arbitrage trade worked as follows. An authorised investor such as a large trading firm would borrow Bitcoin, perhaps by providing US Dollars as collateral to its lender. Using this Bitcoin, they could then subscribe to the Bitcoin Trust, waiting around six months for their shares to be issued. Once GBTC shares were issued, these could then be sold on the market for US Dollars at the premium price. Bitcoin could then be purchased in the spot market and the loan could be repaid. If the premium was 40%, that represents an annualised return of almost 96%. The GBTC premium could therefore be converted into a quasi-interest rate, for the lucky few who were allowed to subscribe. However, remember, one needs to deduct the interest costs of borrowing Bitcoin before one can make a profit. But the Bitcoin interest rate was always quite low, never much more than say 5% and due to the earn model, many retail investors wanted to earn yield on their Bitcoin and there was plenty of supply.

Because the trading firms conducting this trade typically borrowed the Bitcoin, rather than purchasing it, they were never supposed to be exposed to the Bitcoin price during this process. This reduced the risk of the arbitrage trade significantly. The only major risk remaining and it was a very significant risk, was that GBTC loses its premium price within the subscription period. As the premium persisted for many years, this trade was extremely attractive and was one of the major factors driving demand to borrow Bitcoin. The same entities were doing this trade again and again over several years, generating strong returns and using more and more capital and leverage.

Grayscale had other cryptocurrency products and the premium to net asset value in some of these other trusts was even more extreme than Bitcoin. For instance, the Litecoin Trust traded at a peak premium to NAV of 5,871% in late November 2020, according to Bloomberg data. It should be noted that Grayscale's fees are charged on the value of the underlying assets, not the market price of the trusts and therefore the extreme volatility in the premiums of these products does not impact Grayscale's income. Many market analysts blame the Securities and Exchange Commission (SEC) in the United States for the popularity of these flawed products, due to the constant refusal to approve a Bitcoin Exchange Traded Fund (ETF). An ETF would be able to track the price of Bitcoin far more reliably than the non-redeemable trusts.

Genesis Global Trading

When it came to the over the counter (OTC) spot market and the OTC lending market for cryptocurrency trading shops and earn platforms, Genesis Global Trading was considered as the central node and key player. Genesis, is another subsidiary of DCG. Genesis was the largest OTC trading company in the space, facilitating large trades and using spot and derivative exchanges to manage Genesis' exposure and facilitate client demand. Genesis also provided loans across the cryptocurrency ecosystem to various entities. These entities included: proprietary trading shops, hedge funds, market makers, dealers, passive cryptocurrency funds, miners, corporates adding Bitcoin to their treasuries and high net worth individuals. Genesis' early entrance to the market and its parent's strong balance sheet, in part due to Grayscale, made Genesis Global Trading the key trusted financial powerhouse in the cryptocurrency industry. The following chart indicates Genesis' strong growth and success. At the peak in Q4 2021, the company originated almost US$50 billion of loans in just one quarter.

Genesis Global Trading Loan Originations - US$ Billions

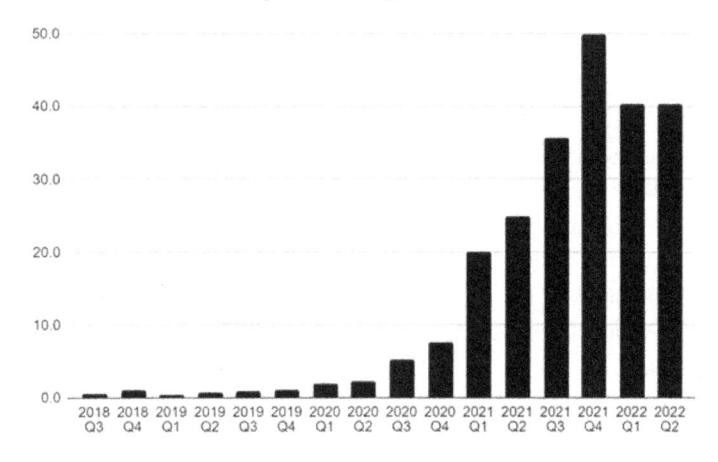

Source: Genesis Global Trading Quarterly Reports

The following chart indicates Genesis' growing balance sheet. At the peak at the end of Q1 2022, the value of loans outstanding stood at almost US$15 billion. It is easy to say with the benefit of hindsight, but the exceptional growth appears to indicate that Genesis' balance sheet expanded too fast.

Genesis Global Trading Outstanding Loan Balance - US$ Billions

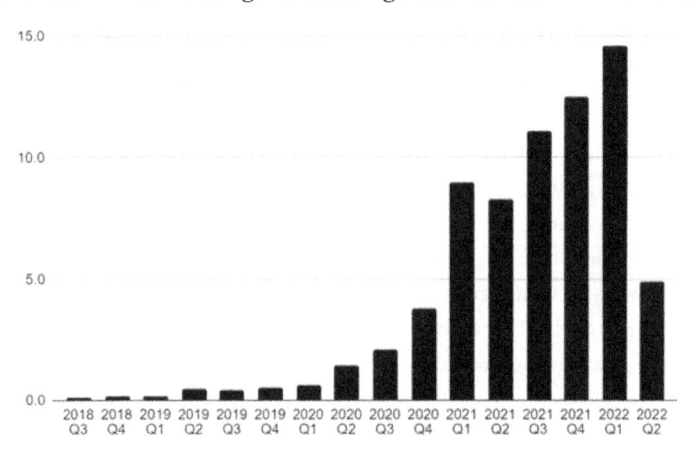

Source: Genesis Global Trading Quarterly Reports

It should be noted that for the most part Genesis did not have trouble financing the loans. There were plenty of counterparties willing to lend Genesis money. If anything, especially with regards to Bitcoin and Ethereum, there was a surplus supply of coins. As Genesis explained in its Q2 2021 market commentary letter:

> *One of the reasons Genesis is able to source cheap BTC and ETH to power our institutional borrowing network is that we are connected to deposit-aggregating retail platforms, including Gemini Earn, Luno, Ledn and BitcoinIRA. These companies provide a gateway for their users to earn yield. We have seen the retail supply side of the market develop much faster than the institutional demand side, with most retail supply in the form of BTC and ETH.[118]*

Genesis Global Trading Loan Book Composition By Coin

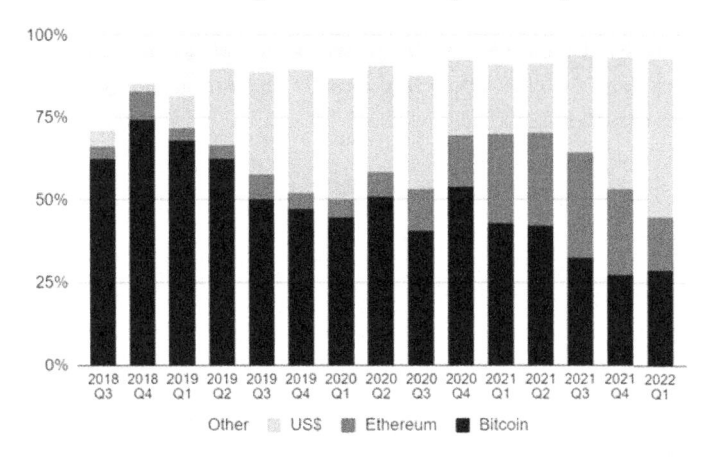

Source: Genesis Global Trading Quarterly Reports

As the chart above indicates, in 2018 there was significant institutional demand to borrow Bitcoin. Almost 75% of Genesis' loan book was Bitcoin. This was driven by demand to use Bitcoin on

---

[118] https://info.genesistrading.com/hubfs/quarterly-reports/2021/q2-2021-report.pdf

trading platforms such as BitMEX and the GBTC trade. One could argue that if the funds were to be used in the GBTC trade there was a potential conflict of interest here, since Genesis and Grayscale were part of the same group of companies. Genesis may have been keener to lend to entities who were creating GBTC units, such that Grayscale could earn higher fee income. On the other hand, while GBTC was trading at a premium, one could also argue that the companies in the group had a responsibility to help improve the quality of the GBTC product and reduce the premium. From this point of view, lending Bitcoin to facilitate the creation of more units of GBTC was legitimate and should have been encouraged.

By 2019 demand to borrow US Dollars began to catch up as the stablecoins began to dominate on the cryptocurrency trading platforms. Bitcoin started losing its crown as the most borrowed institutional currency in the crypto system. Then in early 2021, demand to borrow Ethereum started to grow. It looked as if Ethereum was set to replace Bitcoin as the dominant lending currency. However, by the end of 2021 US Dollar stablecoins showed their strength and overtook both Bitcoin and Ethereum, as the most popular coin for institutional borrowers.

3AC

The next company we will look at, which is crucial in understanding the structure of the lending markets, is the cryptocurrency trading firm and investment fund Three Arrows Capital (3AC). The two co-founders and managers of the fund were Su Zhu and Kyle Davies. Su and Kyle both had careers in the investment banking industry in the Asia Pacific region, working at Deutsche Bank and Credit Suisse respectively. Su was also a trader at FlowTraders, a specialist ETF market maker. In their banking careers, both engaged in arbitrage trading. They both developed skills in profiting from anomalies and discrepancies in prices across various instruments. This is the approach they took to 3AC. They targeted markets with inefficiencies which could be exploited for profit. In particular, inefficiencies which occur again and again so that the profits stack up. In 2012 the pair set up 3AC, not to trade cryptocurrencies, but to engage in trading strategies to take advantage of mispricing in traditional markets. The fund traded primarily with their own capital, which at the time was around US$1.2 million. The area of focus was Non-Deliverable Forward (NDF) contracts.[119] Establishing the banking relationships to trade these instruments could not have been easy and it's impressive that 3AC managed to get all the necessary accounts set up. 3AC appears to have been quite successful with this strategy for a number of years.

After a few years, perhaps by around 2017, 3AC started to deploy capital into the cryptocurrency space. The first strategy they deployed is likely to be going short Bitcoin in the perpetual swap contract and earning the funding rate. Bitcoin and cryptocurrency is of course alluring to many and 3AC appeared to have caught the bug. At some point they began to build long positions on tokens and companies in the ecosystem. Su Zhu established himself as one of the thought leaders in the cryptocurrency space. He had strong knowledge about Ethereum and was a host on the popular Uncommon Core cryptocurrency podcast, with industry analyst Hasu. There they had in depth discussions about various issues such as the cultural state of the Ethereum community. Su was clearly intelligent. This helped boost the brand and reputation of 3AC, who established themselves as one of the smartest, most trusted, well capitalised and well-connected companies in the cryptocurrency space.

In order to improve the return on equity for the fund holders, at some point 3AC began to borrow capital. When the fund borrowed capital, it paid the lender in the form of interest, however the lenders did not have a stake in the profits of the fund. As long as the investment returns were above the interest rates, investors in the fund got improved returns. Therefore, while borrowing may be appealing to 3AC, it is not clear if it was the best decision from the point of view of the lenders. One could argue it was a heads they win, tails you lose

---

[119] https://blog.bitmex.com/number-three/

type situation. If the bets win, 3AC equity holders get better returns, if the bets lose, lenders may not get their money back. On the other hand, 3AC was not expected to lose. They were the smart guys in the space and knew what they were doing. There was also a view that 3AC were primarily engaged in market neutral trading strategies, bets that would work regardless of which direction cryptocurrency prices moved. In the bull market of 2021, 3AC was successful and is likely to have had strong returns. At its peak, the group's AuM is believed to be as high as US$10 billion or US$18 billion according to some sources.[120][121]

The GBTC Trade

The most significant trading strategy 3AC participated in was the GBTC trade, mentioned earlier in this chapter. A trade they could repeat again and again and earn handsome returns. Su and Kyle had demonstrated their hustling capabilities in the NDF market and now they appeared to have a strong and lucrative relationship with Grayscale. However, the GBTC trade is risky, because while the trust traded at a premium to NAV for years, it could lose the premium and trade at a discount. There were rumours circulating in the industry, which speculated that 3AC somehow had some clever way of conducting the GBTC trade, while mitigating or eliminating the risk, perhaps due to a special arrangement with Grayscale. Exactly how this could be achieved was never clear and with the benefit of hindsight, it is unlikely 3AC did successfully mitigate this risk.

According to regulatory filings, which may be slightly unreliable, especially with regards to the exact dates of the positions, 3AC held 39 million units of GBTC. This represents around 5.7% of outstanding units in the trust. The market valuation of this holding, at the peak, may have been around US$2.3 billion. This made 3AC the largest investor in GBTC. This is larger than the holding of Cathie Wood's Ark ETF funds, which had a peak holding of around 18

---

[120] https://www.bloomberg.com/news/articles/2022-04-07/three-arrows-capital-s-su-zhu-remains-bullish-on-crypto-investments
[121] https://coingape.com/everything-about-three-arrows-capitals-insolvency-risks-and-what-happened/

million units, according to data from Bloomberg. This trade was financed, in large part, by Genesis. 3AC was even able to obtain these loans from Genesis, in part, by placing units of GBTC up as collateral. The timing of the creation of the units is not entirely clear and it's not easy to determine if 3AC had exposure to Bitcoin or if it was always hedged. However, given that GBTC units were used as collateral, to conduct a trade which depended on the premium of GBTC, it seems the risks here may be even more elevated.

At the end of February 2021 GBTC switched from trading at a premium to a discount. It is not clear exactly what caused this, be it the plethora of alternative Bitcoin exchange traded products that launched in the year or the emergence of MicroStrategy [MSTR] as a listed proxy for Bitcoin which may have contributed. Whatever the reason, GBTC now traded at a discount to the underlying Bitcoin and the discount was getting larger and larger. This is likely to have been very painful for 3AC and the other funds conducting the GBTC trade. Even if 3AC did not lose that much money as a result of the discount, they certainly lost a lucrative trading strategy.

In early June 2022, 3AC were raising money for a new investment strategy. Again, taking advantage of the mispricing of GBTC, which was at this time trading at a 33% discount. 3AC was asking investors to provide Bitcoin and if the discount closed, then the fund would make profits.[122] This trade was even more simple, all one had to do was borrow Bitcoin and buy GBTC in the market. The discount could close to zero if the SEC allowed the trust to convert to an ETF. The investors would this time share some of the upsides of the strategy, after paying 3AC a large performance fee. Just as before, rumours were circulating that 3AC had a strong relationship with Grayscale and that this could somehow mitigate the risks of the trade. Rumours about 3AC's superior knowledge about the likelihood of SEC approval of a Bitcoin ETF also circulated among potential investors. With the benefit of hindsight, these rumours were probably untrue.

---

[122] https://www.theblock.co/post/152735/three-arrows-capital-team-sought-funds-for-gbtc-trade-before-meltdown

The Luna Trade

Another core investment strategy for 3AC was Luna and a trade linked with the associated stablecoin UST. At the start of 2022, 3AC invested US$200 million into Luna, providing capital for the LFG.[123] The total value of the investment in Luna is believed to be around US$600 million.[124] Su Zhu was also said to be close friends with the Luna founder Do Kwon. Su talked of his closeness to Do and how he believed that Luna was "going to do big things". Do can be considered as a persuasive, confident and articulate individual and his powers of persuasion appeared to have had an impact on Su Zhu.

The UST trade was incredibly simple. All 3AC had to do was borrow USDC from their counterparties at around 6% to 12% and then convert the USDC into UST. The UST could then be deployed into the Anchor protocol, earning 20%. Given the leverage involved the returns to Su and Kyle must have been extremely attractive. With this trade being so simple, one could ask why the lenders were prepared to finance this, rather than doing it themselves.

Simplicity

For all the excitement in the market about DeFi, the main structure of the crypto credit market was reasonably simple. It can be described, in a highly simplified form, as follows:

1. Retail customers placed coins on deposit at the earn platforms.
2. The earn platforms lent coins to Genesis.
3. Genesis then lent the money to 3AC.
4. 3AC then deployed the funds into the GBTC trade or into the Anchor protocol.

---

[123] https://www.wsj.com/articles/battered-crypto-hedge-fund-three-arrows-capital-considers-asset-sales-bailout-11655469932
[124] https://cointelegraph.com/news/3ac-founders-reveal-ties-to-terra-founder-blame-overconfidence-for-collapse

Flow of funds in the crypto credit market

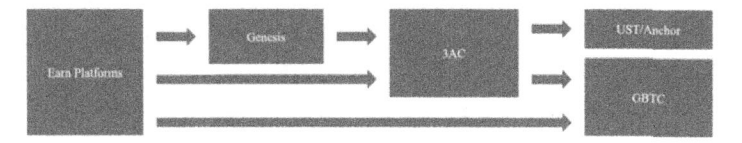

Some of the earn platforms bypassed Genesis, going straight to 3AC. Examples of this include companies such as Voyager and Celsius, who directly lent the customer deposits out to 3AC, rather than going through Genesis. BlockFi even bypassed both Genesis and 3AC and engaged in the GBTC trade directly itself. Of course, the above model is an oversimplification and funds were also lent to other counterparties.

This is not to say the entire earn business model was flawed. Many of the customer funds were lent out, either directly or indirectly, to high quality genuinely market neutral crypto currency market makers and arbitrage funds. A market neutral fund can generate positive returns whether markets are moving upwards or downwards, because they are conducting price arbitrage or other strategies which don't depend on price trends. However, one can argue that even the best of these market neutral funds require a lot of retail investment flow to generate these solid low risk returns at scale. Therefore, sophisticated and well-run funds can earn high returns in a cryptocurrency bull market when retail money is flowing into the space in a frenzied fashion. Then, when the markets calm down and the bull market ends, the investment returns of these funds should gracefully decline towards zero, due to a lack of arbitrage opportunities, without losing any money at all. These funds could then return the capital to the earn platforms, who could then lower the yields provided to their customers. The customers could then withdraw, without anyone losing any money. There were many well managed funds in the space that were genuinely market neutral and there were some high quality earn platforms that only lent to these funds.

It is possible the earn market could have been constructed entirely in this robust and safe fashion. However, this did not occur. Some of the investment funds became greedy and complacent in the bull market. Not all of them were as market neutral as they claimed and some didn't even claim to be totally market neutral. At the same time some of the earn businesses became complacent with their lending standards. Again, perhaps influenced by greed and DeFi related hype.

As the bull market continued, the exposure and the sizes of the balance sheets grew and grew. There was significant risk in the system and retail was exposed to that. For the most part that risk was traditional in nature, with many similarities to the 2008 global financial crisis. It was not the genuine DeFi projects that were the epicentre of risk, which is what many analysts had thought, but the same old mistakes that happen in finance again and again. There was bad risk management, too much leverage, poor incentives, too much greed, too many conflicts of interests, insufficient regulation when taking retail deposits and the proliferation of unsustainable investment strategies. It was no longer a question of if the bubble will pop, but when? And the sooner it happened the better, because the longer the bubble lasted, the more retail investors could get hurt.

15

Financial Contagion

The Luna Collapse

On 9th May 2022, the UST stablecoin began to lose its peg. It reached a low of US$0.79 on the day. Remember, the coin was constructed such that if it traded below US$1, new Luna tokens would automatically be issued out of nothing to prop up the price of UST. This structure created a potential opportunity for hedge funds, who could first short or borrow Luna and then short or dump UST, profiting when the Luna price declines because of the new issuance hitting the market. As UST lost its peg, rumours were circulating that a large sophisticated fund was conducting this exact trade. The so-called Soros style attack Do Kwon had called the "most retarded" idea.[125] There was significant speculation inside the cryptocurrency community about which hedge fund this might be, including rumours about Ken Griffin's Citadel Securities or investment management giant Blackrock.[126] It is of course extremely unlikely that anyone associated with these entities was involved. If there was a hedge fund with a large balance sheet conducting this trade, it was likely a cryptocurrency specialist trading firm or former employees of one of these large firms.

Most traders did not seem to believe the intention of the short seller was to break UST completely. The plan could have been to cause it to trade at a significant discount, then cover the position. UST could then recover back to US$1. However, on 10th May 2022, UST

---

[125] https://twitter.com/stablekwon/status/1464897977793728514
[126] https://www.youtube.com/watch?v=g3eaQF-keek

continued to crash, reaching a low of US$0.68. The coin was incredibly volatile, trading as high as US$0.94 on the day. Many market participants now believed that the integrity of UST had been ruined and a recovery was unlikely. UST continued its price decline, on 11th May it traded between US$0.30 and US$0.85. Then by Saturday 14th May, it was all over, UST traded between US$0.14 and US$0.25. The coin remained extremely volatile, but continued its decline towards a price of a few cents, which it trades at today.

The UST failure was in spite of an attempted defence by the LFG, which used up its reserves. On 7th May 2022, the LFG had over US$3 billion in reserves, including over 80,000 Bitcoin. By 11th May 2022, this had plummeted to just over US$100 million.[127]

This was all bad news for Luna, whose supply was skyrocketing as the system tried to maintain the US Dollar peg. The price of Luna was therefore plummeting. On the 5th May 2022, the price of Luna was around US$85 per coin, a market capitalisation of around US$30 billion. In this period, unsurprisingly the price of the coin crashed and on 11th May Luna reached a low of $0.85, before continuing its decline to a fraction of a cent, which it trades at today. Luna was seen as one of the hottest coins of 2022 and it was incredibly painful for many investors who were totally wiped out in just a few days. Almost US$30 billion of apparent value, up in smoke in a few days.

On around the 11th May 2022, it also emerged that Do Kwon was behind a stablecoin project called Basis Cash, which launched in 2017 and then collapsed.[128] Do had used the pseudonym "Rick Sanchez" from the TV show Rick and Morty. Many UST investors were concerned by this, especially because it was not disclosed to them before they invested in UST. This was more painful for some investors as in a Tweet in December 2020, Do appears to criticise Basis Cash, calling it a "zero sum game", while indicating UST was the "king".[129]

---

[127] https://dashboard.lfg.org/
[128] https://cryptobriefing.com/do-kwon-outed-basis-cash/
[129] https://twitter.com/stablekwon/status/1344273369219223557

The failure of Luna caused a wider decline in cryptocurrency prices. Bitcoin fell from around US$40,000 to US$30,000, while Ethereum fell from US$3,000 to US$2,000 in the period. The failure of UST and Luna caused panic in some sections of the industry, as they did not know which counterparties had exposure and who to trust. In mid-June, about a month later, the market took another leg down. Bitcoin crashed from US$30,000 to US$20,000 and Ethereum fell to below US$1,000.

On Tuesday 14th June 2022, rumours started to circulate that 3AC was in trouble. 3AC had lost funds on the GBTC trade and had been a large supporter of Luna. Many counterparties had exposure to 3AC and they began to call back their loans. Many were observing 3AC's known DeFi wallets on the Ethereum blockchain, assessing how they managed their leverage and exposure.

DeFi Demonstrates Its Advantages

In general, the DeFi platforms appeared to perform well in this crisis, just like the performance in the May 2021 crash a year earlier. If a trading firm was struggling to obtain the liquidity it needed to make margin calls, it would pay its DeFi obligations first. This is because these positions in DeFi are transparent and if the company wanted to avoid spreading panic about its solvency, it had to make these public positions a priority. Nobody wanted to get liquidated in DeFi, where everyone could see the liquidation in real time.

Actually, not many liquidations occurred in June 2022 on the major Ethereum DeFi contracts, only around US$150 million on Compound. By and large, the leveraged DeFi positions were successfully unwound. Although the level of liquidations were small, the value of outstanding debt sharply declined and the interest rates also plummeted. Debt on Compound declined from around US$8 billion at the start of the year to US$800 million at the end of June

2022. In the same period, the US Dollar borrow rate declined to around 1% to 2% on Compound.

3AC Bankruptcy

After failing to meet margin calls and failing to pay its creditors, in July 2022 3AC filed for bankruptcy. The creditors then came forward to make claims and analysts started to learn more details. It looked like there were around US$4 billion of claims on 3AC's assets, with the largest claims listed below. However, some lenders may have had collateral placed with them to secure the loans. Therefore, the final bill for 3AC may be lower than the figures in the below table.

3AC Creditor	US$ Millions
Genesis	2,360.3
Voyager	685.5
Blockchain.com*	270.0
Equities First	162.1
Deribit	80.0
Celsius	75.3
FalconX	65.5
DRB	51.1
Coinlist	35.0
Ashla	21.0
BitMEX	20.0

Source: 3AC legal liquidation documents, Reuters
Notes: In the case of many of the lenders, they may have collateral placed with them which may have been liquidated, therefore the amount of debt outstanding may be lower than the amounts stated above.
* In the case of Blockchain.com, the US$270 million figure may be the value of the deficit after liquidation on a larger loan.

3AC had borrowed a huge amount of money from across the ecosystem, although most of the loans originated from the earn platforms, either directly or indirectly. It is possible that there are other large debts not in the previous table, with some counterparties not wanting to make their potential losses public.

The failure of 3AC caused issues for several large creditors. We will discuss the challenges some of these large creditors faced in the coming chapters.

Earn platform and crypto lender Matrix Port was revealed to be another large creditor of 3AC, however it is not clear what amount is owed.[130] The company is backed by Jihan Wu, the co-founder of Bitmain (A large Bitcoin mining machine manufacturer). At the time of writing, it does not appear that 3ACs failure caused solvency problems for Matrix Port.

The well-known Bitcoin wallet and block explorer company Blockchain.com (originally called Blockchain.info), may have lent up to US$700 million to 3AC and US$270 million of which may have been outstanding at the time of bankruptcy.[131] Just a few months earlier in March 2022, according to Bloomberg,[132] blockchain.com raised money from Lightspeed Ventures and Baillie Gifford at an astonishing US$14 billion valuation. The highly respected Edinburgh based asset manager topped up, following its US$100 million investment in the company in 2021.[133] Blockchain.com also raised money from well-known macro investors Louis Bacon and Kyle Bass.[134] It appeared as if Blockchain.com deployed a significant proportion of the funds it raised, in the form of loans to 3AC. It is not clear if this is what the investors in the company had intended. It is possible that Blockchain.com considered this as a reasonably safe short-term deposit, rather than a high risk investment.

---

[130] https://wublock.substack.com/p/who-lent-money-to-three-arrows-capital
[131] https://www.reuters.com/technology/blockchaincom-faces-270-mln-hit-loans-bankrupt-three-arrows-coindesk-2022-07-08/
[132] https://www.bloomberg.com/news/articles/2022-03-30/blockchain-com-in-talks-for-new-funding-at-14-billion-valuation
[133] https://decrypt.co/68595/baillie-gifford-invests-100-million-into-blockchain-com
[134] https://medium.com/blockchain/blockchain-com-raised-120m-strategic-growth-round-led-by-macro-investors-84488f4a0913

Blockchain.com never appeared insolvent as a result of the losses and in October 2022 the company conducted a further funding round from UK based investment manager Kingsway Capital.[135] The valuation of this deal is likely to be far lower than the US$14 billion figure achieved a few months earlier.

Genesis

Genesis was the largest 3AC creditor, with loans perhaps related to the GBTC trade. The loan was partly collateralised by GBTC units pledged to Genesis. The solvency of Genesis never appeared to be under threat, given the backing of its parent, DCG. However, in the aftermath of this crisis, the CEO of Genesis, Michael Moro stepped down and there were widespread redundancies at the firm, with the headcount declining by 20%.[136]

The failure of 3AC was probably the most significant in terms of scale and it sent shockwaves across the rest of the cryptocurrency credit system. Platforms, trading shops and retail investors across the space demanded liquidity in the panic. Bitcoin was an important asset traders wanted to custody, however USDC was the ultimate asset people needed to get their hands on. Not unlike the global financial crisis in 2008, in a few weeks sentiment had shifted, from excitement and greed, to fear and panic.

---

[135] https://medium.com/blockchain/welcoming-kingsway-capital-2cd3a1805c25
[136] https://www.bloomberg.com/news/articles/2022-08-17/genesis-ceo-steps-down-as-crypto-broker-slashes-its-workforce

16

The Earn Collapse

Voyager

Another leading earn platform, Voyager, is somewhat unique, in that it was a public company. The company was listed in Canada. Therefore, Voyager's quarterly financial statements are available for financial analysts to evaluate and the level of disclosure is much higher than for other earn platform entities. Voyager was also a large 3AC creditor, the largest 3AC earn platform creditor and this resulted in the Voyager's bankruptcy.

Before the collapse, at the end of March 2022, Voyager's balance sheet was around US$6 billion in size. The company had crypto assets payable to customers of US$5.5 billion (or US$5.7bn of liabilities when including cryptocurrency is held as collateral). This resulted in a positive equity position of US$257 million. This was a leverage ratio of 23.3 to 1, or in other words a write down of 4.3% of the assets would wipe out all the group's equity, which feels quite risky given the risk profile of the assets.

It is important to clarify the types of risks these earn platforms need to manage. There are four primary asset management risks:

- **Asset matching:** Given the high volatility in cryptocurrency prices, it is important the value of coins in the assets and liabilities match. For example, taking customer deposits in a volatile dog meme coin like Dogecoin and converting this to

USDC so that the Dollars can be lent out and earn a yield is very risky.

- **Duration risk:** It is important the duration of the assets are not too long compared to the duration of the liabilities. Customer deposits grew very quickly and therefore it is probably good to assume they could be quickly withdrawn in certain scenarios. The earn platforms need to ensure that they have sufficient liquidity on hand to meet withdrawals and that the assets are not locked up in protocols or lent out for long durations. If the mismatch is too large, the platform could have insufficient liquidity and be unable to process withdrawals.

- **Counterparty risk:** The earn platform needs to ensure that it has sufficient diversification with respect to its credit counterparties. Ideally, the platform should not be too exposed to any one borrower, such that if the largest borrower defaults the platform is still solvent.

- **Interest rate spread:** It is also sensible to ensure that interest rates are set such that there is a positive spread between the average lending rate and the average deposit rate, such that the company is profitable and able to build equity.

In general, in this crisis, the most common mistake the earn platforms made was having inappropriate risk controls with respect to both asset duration and managing counterparty exposure. A negative net interest margin was also a common mistake.

With the details provided by Voyager in their quarterly disclosures, one is able to dig further into the earn business model. Voyager disclosed the details of the cryptocurrency liabilities due to its customers by coin, as well as the coins it held under its own custody system. The company also disclosed the coins it loaned out. This data is summarised in the table below.

Voyager Balance Sheet Data - As at 31 March 2022 - US$ millions

	Customer Deposits	Assets Held	Loaned Out	Earn Rate
Bitcoin	1,496	1,146	379	4.1%
USDC	842	167	633	9.0%
Ethereum	801	196	629	4.3%
Cardano	307	311		4.0%
Voyager Coin	295	307		7.0%
Shiba Inu	245	211		1.0%
Luna	218		212	4.0%
Dot	137	135		12.0%
Solana	101	101		3.0%
Others	1,040	859	169	
Total	**5,482**	**3,433**	**2,022**	

Source: Voyager financial statements,
https://web.archive.org/web/20220227113941/https://www.investvoyager.com/earn
Note: Earn rate as at the end of February 2022

The data indicates that while Bitcoin was the most popular asset for customers, USDC and Ethereum appear to have been the easiest assets to deploy and loan out, due to demand to borrow these tokens. 76% of the client Bitcoin remained static inside Voyager, the comparable figure for Ethereum was just 24%. In contrast, highly speculative alternative coins such as Shiba Inu (A dog meme related coin) and Voyager Coin (The native token of its own platform), did not appear to be lent out at all. This is likely due to a lack of demand from borrowers and a lack of utility of these coins. As a result of this, the customer earn rate on Shiba Inu was low, at 1% in March 2022. However, it is not clear how this 1% yield was funded. The exception here is Luna, which was almost 100% loaned out.

Cardano, Dot and Solana are proof of stake blockchains. Therefore, the coins could be used for staking and earn a yield natively on their own blockchains, without being lent out. These staking networks normally have a fixed withdrawal period, of say a few weeks, therefore managing the duration of these assets is relatively simple.

Voyager also provided a breakdown of the borrowers and a range of interest rates they could obtain, without disclosing the names of the entities. This data is summarised in the table below.

Borrower	Interest Rate	Amount - US$m
BVI based counterparty	1.0% to 7.5%	728
Singapore based counterparty	2.0% to 9.0%	326
US based counterparty	4.0% to 13.5%	295
UK based counterparty	1.0% to 15.0%	252
Canada based counterparty	1.0% to 30.0%	141
US based counterparty	0.5% to 8.9%	119
US based counterparty	1.0% to 10.0%	35
Other		125
Total		**2,022**

Source: Voyager financial statements
Note: Data as at 31 March 2022

The counterparty concentration risk did seem high. If any one of the top four counterparties failed, Voyager was at risk of insolvency. It is now known that the largest counterparty, with a US$728 million loan balance, was 3AC. Amazingly, 3AC appears to have been given unsecured credit.[137] This means that 3AC did not need to post any asset as collateral. This is in contrast for example, to the loans provided to 3AC by Genesis, which had 80% collateral. BlockFi also lent 3AC money before the insolvency, however these loans were

---

[137] https://wublock.substack.com/p/reveal-the-secrets-of-3ac-1-billion

over collateralised, perhaps at 133%.[138] Over collateralisation is necessary due to the volatility of the underlying assets. Lending 3AC such a large proportion of the balance sheet, in an unsecured way, appears to be extremely irresponsible. In the crisis, in May and June 2022, concerns were raised about Voyager's solvency and there was a deposit run.

On 18th June 2022, it was announced that a US$200 million and 15,000 Bitcoin credit line may be provided to Voyager by Alameda Research, with a 5% interest rate.[139] Alameda Research is the trading arm of the cryptocurrency exchange FTX. Alameda was regarded as a large, sophisticated and successful proprietary trading shop. The trading shop is said to have made up to ten times more money than FTX in 2021, up to US$10 million per day in some periods. However, these were only rumours and the profitability of Alameda was never clear. The "non-binding" credit line with Alameda was designed to give depositors confidence and perhaps stop the panic. It could also provide much needed liquidity. However, the announcement said the agreement was not definitive. Ultimately the announcement did not work. On 1st July 2022, Voyager announced that it was suspending withdrawals, blaming the default of 3AC and "market conditions".

> *Voyager, announced it is temporarily suspending trading, deposits, withdrawals and loyalty rewards, effective at 2:00 p.m. Eastern Daylight Time today. "This was a tremendously difficult decision, but we believe it is the right one given current market conditions," said Stephen Ehrlich, Chief Executive Officer of Voyager. "This decision gives us additional time to continue exploring strategic alternatives with various interested parties while preserving the value of the Voyager platform we have built together. We will provide additional information at the appropriate time." Voyager previously announced that its subsidiary,*

---

[138] https://onthebrink-podcast.com/blockfi-jun22/
[139] https://www.prnewswire.com/news-releases/voyager-digital-signs-term-sheet-for-us200-million-and-15-000-btc-revolving-line-of-credit-with-alameda-research-301570656.html

> *Voyager Digital LLC, issued a notice of default to Three Arrows Capital ("3AC") for failure to make the required payments on its previously disclosed loan of 15,250 BTC and $350 million USDC. Voyager is actively pursuing all available remedies for recovery from 3AC, including through the court-ordered liquidation process in the British Virgin Islands.[140]*

A few days later, on the 5th July 2022, the company announced that it had started the bankruptcy process.[141] On 26th September 2022, Voyager announced that FTX had won an auction to acquire the cryptocurrency assets of the company for US$1.4 billion.[142] At the time the fair market price of the assets was US$1.3 billion and the loan to 3AC was excluded from the purchase. This deal should provide liquidity to distribute assets to Voyager's creditors. Alameda Research was revealed to be the largest creditor of Voyager, with an unsecured US$75 million loan.[143] Alameda also returned US$200 million of crypto assets to Voyager on 12th September 2022 and in return Voyager released collateral in the form of tokens associated with FTX, such as the exchange's FTT token.[144] This loan deal originated in September 2021. With this existing complex relationship with FTX, with a web of loans in both directions, it perhaps made sense that FTX helped provide the group with liquidity during the bankruptcy. Such a complex relationship with FTX did appear to be a little strange, however at the time not many people questioned FTX's solvency.

After the Voyager bankruptcy, many of the depositors indicated that they believed Voyager had behaved in an unethical manner and misled investors. Legal action was launched by depositors who made several accusations.[145]

---

[140] https://www.newswire.ca/news-releases/voyager-digital-provides-market-update-851734302.html
[141] https://www.prnewswire.com/news-releases/voyager-digital-commences-financial-restructuring-process-to-maximize-value-for-all-stakeholders-301581177.html
[142] https://www.prnewswire.com/news-releases/voyager-completes-successful-auction-and-announces-agreement-for-ftx-to-acquire-its-assets-301633679.html
[143] https://decrypt.co/110218/binance-and-ftx-lead-50m-race-to-purchase-voyagers-assets-report
[144] https://cases.stretto.com/public/x193/11753/PLEADINGS/1175309202280000000002.pdf
[145] https://www.classaction.org/media/cassidy-v-voyager-digital-ltd-et-al.pdf

The Earn Collapse

- The lawsuit alleges that Voyager claimed to offer 100% commission free trading, but actually charged "exorbitant hidden commissions on every cryptocurrency trade".
- The lawsuit also alleges that Voyager had an inappropriate partnership with the Dallas Mavericks Basketball team which is owned by Mark Cuban.[146] The plaintiff's claim that in a video conference with fans, Mark Cuban said the "Voyager platform makes the process [of investing in digital currencies] easy and simplified for fans of all ages". Which the plaintiff argues was inappropriate promotion to those with "limited funds and experience".

Voyager has also been accused of making misleading statements about the degree to which their customers were protected by FDIC insurance. In a now deleted Tweet from November 2020, Voyager stated:

> *Have you heard? USD held with Voyager is FDIC insured up to $250K. Our customers' security is our top priority. Start growing your crypto portfolio today.*[147]

After the bankruptcy, The Federal Reserve put out a press release with a warning, indicating that the statement from Voyager about the FDIC insurance may be misleading.

> *Voyager and certain officers and employees made various statements online, including on its website, mobile app, and social media accounts, stating or suggesting that: Voyager itself is FDIC-insured; Customers who invested with the Voyager cryptocurrency platform would receive FDIC insurance coverage for all funds provided to, and held by, Voyager, without reference to the insured depository institution account; and The FDIC would insure*

---

[146] https://www.mavs.com/mavsvoyager/
[147] https://archive.ph/kbUGU#selection-627.0-627.154

customers against the failure of Voyager itself. These representations are false and misleading.[148]

At the time of writing, Voyager's reputation appears to be in tatters and customers are understandably furious at the management team. However, Voyager was not the only earn business to fail.

Other Insolvent Earn Platforms

In the aftermath of the crash, bankruptcies and financial contagion, several other earn businesses suspended withdrawals. This book will not cover all of them in detail. Other earn platforms which failed include Babel and Hodlnaut:

- **Babel** - Hong Kong based Babel Finance suspended withdrawals on 17 June 2022. At the end of 2021, the platform is said to have had customer deposits of over US$3 billion. Just one month before the suspension of withdrawals, Babel raised US$80 million in funding at a US$2 billion valuation.[149] [150]
- **Hodlnaut**[151] - On 8th August 2022, the Singapore based firm announced it was suspending withdrawals. On 30th August, the firm was placed in bankruptcy. On 16th June 2022, the company announced that it had zero exposure to 3AC.[152] Hodlnaut is believed to have had client assets in the US$350 million range. In April 2022, Hodlnaut added support for UST deposits, offering a yield of 13% of 14% if the funds were locked up for 180 days.[153] The company is said to have had exposure to Anchor and UST[154] and therefore became insolvent. Just a few months prior to this, in March 2022, Hodlnaut received an In-Principle Approval

---

[148] https://www.federalreserve.gov/newsevents/pressreleases/bcreg20220728a.htm
[149] https://www.cnbc.com/2022/06/17/babel-finance-suspends-withdrawals-as-crypto-markets-slump.html
[150] https://www.coindesk.com/business/2022/06/17/babel-finance-suspends-withdrawals-citing-unusual-liquidity-pressures/
[151] https://www.hodlnaut.com/press/hodlnaut-message-to-our-users
[152] https://twitter.com/hodlnautdotcom/status/1537464442752888832
[153] https://twitter.com/FatManTerra/status/1541101957779177472
[154] https://twitter.com/FatManTerra/status/1541101980806004738

(IPA) from the Monetary Authority of Singapore (MAS) for a Major Payment Institution License.[155]

Other smaller earn platforms that suspended withdrawals include Vauld,[156] Freeway[157] and BlueBenx.[158]

CoinFlex

Another company that suspended withdrawals during the period was the cryptocurrency derivatives exchange CoinFlex. However, it is difficult to characterise this as an earn related collapse. If anything, Coinflex's problems can be seen as a remnant of the 2017/18 era issues facing the cryptocurrency space, namely The Blocksize War.

On 23rd June 2022, CoinFlex announced that it was suspending withdrawals, due to "extreme market conditions last week & continued uncertainty involving a counterparty".[159] The company indicated that the counterparty was not 3AC. Then on the 27th June 2022, CoinFlex put out another astonishing statement,[160] which indicated the following:

- The exchange was insolvent, because one large customer had used leverage and gone into negative equity.
- In normal circumstances, CoinFlex would not allow such a negative balance and would liquidate the position, however, this individual had a "non-liquidation recourse account" due to "stringent personal guarantees".
- As a solution, repeating the Bitfinex playbook of 2016 and 2019, CoinFlex was to launch a recovery token, rvUSD, to monetize this individual's debt.

---

[155] https://www.prnewswire.com/news-releases/cryptocurrency-firm-hodlnaut-receives-in-principle-approval-ipa-from-the-monetary-authority-of-singapore-mas-301502707.html
[156] https://www.bloomberg.com/news/articles/2022-07-05/troubled-crypto-lender-vauld-says-it-may-get-acquired-by-nexo
[157] https://cryptoslate.com/freeway-halts-withdrawals-fatmanterra-alleges-ponzi-scheme/
[158] https://cointelegraph.com/news/bluebenx-fires-employees-halts-funds-withdrawal-citing-32m-hack
[159] https://coinflex.com/blog/coinflex-update-on-withdrawals/
[160] https://coinflex.com/blog/coinflexs-solution-to-resume-withdrawls/

It quickly emerged that this individual was Roger Ver, one of the early investors in CoinFlex. In a kind of joke, the "rv" stood for both "recovery value" and Roger Ver. It appeared to emerge that the debt was related to a large margin long position on a coin called Bitcoin Cash, believed to be as large as 0.5 million coins. By 9th July 2022, CoinFlex indicated that the position was liquidated, resulting in a shortfall of US$84 million.[161] This debt was so large that the exchange did not have enough liquidity to process withdrawals. For his part, Roger Ver denied owing the exchange any money, stating on Twitter:

> *Recently some rumours have been spreading that I have defaulted on a debt to a counterparty. These rumours are false. Not only do I not have a debt to this counterparty, but this counter-party owes me a substantial sum of money, and I am currently seeking the return of my funds.*[162]

It seems that both sides may have had a different interpretation of the terms of the special non-recourse account. Bitcoin Cash was a token which spun-off from Bitcoin in 2017, after a long and confrontational dispute and Roger Ver had been a key advocate for the new coin. CoinFlex was an exchange which was a significant supporter of Bitcoin Cash. In an unexpected final chapter to the five year old dispute in Bitcoin, one of the main characters on the Bitcoin Cash side, appears to have been hit by the market turmoil of 2022. Roger Ver certainly put his money where his mouth was, still attempting to maintain a margin long position in Bitcoin Cash all these years later. However, some market participants may argue it was not fair that his account was special and couldn't be liquidated, resulting in him having a potential advantage over the traders on the other side of the book to him. At least the existence of such an account should have been disclosed to the traders.

---

[161] https://coinflex.com/blog/coinflex-update-july-9-2022/
[162] https://twitter.com/rogerkver/status/1541822377461415936

Blockfi

In the crisis, the darling of the earn industry, BlockFi, certainly performed better than rival platforms such as Voyager. BlockFi said it had no outstanding positions with 3AC. It did lend to 3AC in the past, however these positions were over collateralised. BlockFi also announced it was totally out of the GBTC trade.[163] BlockFi had been a major player in the GBTC trade in the past, however with GBTC trading at a discount this trade was no longer possible.

BlockFi was still in a serious crisis though, because due to the failure of other earn platforms, its customers were panicking and withdrawing. In the heart of the storm, the CEO Zac Prince said in an interview that BlockFi received withdrawal requests amounting to 10% of the deposit balance per day. However, BlockFi was able to handle this without suspending withdrawals.

To try and put a stop to the panic, just like Voyager, BlockFi announced a deal with FTX. On 21st June 2022, Zac Prince announced the following on Twitter:

> *Today @BlockFi signed a term sheet with @FTX_Official to secure a $250M revolving credit facility providing us with access to capital that further bolsters our balance sheet and platform strength.*[164]

This was a week after the announcement of the revolving credit line between Alameda and Voyager. Again, this announcement appeared to be a move designed to calm depositors, but the agreement with FTX did not appear to be fully executed. FTX had established itself as a lender of last resort to troubled cryptocurrency lenders. Rightly or wrongly, FTX was regarded as one of the most profitable companies in the space and it had taken on an almost central bank type role, apparently for the good of the industry.

---
[163] https://twitter.com/BlockFiZac/status/1546609720051499016
[164] https://twitter.com/BlockFiZac/status/1539216594383028224

Some of BlockFi's investors regarded the deal with FTX as controversial. Another investor in BlockFi, Morgan Creek, was trying to raise capital for a rival bailout offer.[165] According to a partner at Morgan Creek, the FTX credit line gave FTX the option to buy BlockFi "at essentially zero price", which would wipe out all other equity investors. This perhaps indicates that BlockFi was worried about liquidity and failing to meet withdrawal requests. This was emergency funding and protecting depositors, rather than investors in BlockFi equity was the priority. On 1st July 2022, BlockFi finally agreed terms with FTX.[166] The eventual size of the revolving credit facility was US$400 million. This deal is also said to have included the option for FTX to acquire the company, at a value of around US$150 million, according to the Financial Times. This deal did protect depositors, however for BlockFi investors, who had valued the company at up to US$4.5 billion, this was surely a painful moment. With the company raising US$1 billion in investor capital, it is quite remarkable that BlockFi seemed to run out of cash so quickly. This is probably partly explained by a duration mismatch in BlockFi's assets and liabilities.

At the end of August 2022, SBF implied in an interview with Bloomberg that the bailouts had mixed results.[167]

> *I think some were going to turn out to be profitable, some won't be. We had to make snap judgement calls. With Voyager, I think there's $70 million there that we put in that I'm not sure we're ever seeing again. [BlockFi] just sort of burned through their runway, had a functional business with a strong team and just needed more cash to be able to operate effectively going forward.*

---

[165] https://www.coindesk.com/business/2022/06/25/morgan-creek-is-trying-to-counter-ftxs-blockfi-bailout-leaked-call-shows/
[166] https://www.ft.com/content/fa95d027-8afd-43f1-b9b1-ee8c204435c7
[167] https://www.bloomberg.com/news/articles/2022-08-31/sam-bankman-fried-crypto-bailouts-had-mixed-results

SBF is said to have indicated that perhaps he regrets the Voyager bailout, however he was happy with the decision to bailout BlockFi. As to whether FTX really had the balance sheet strength to bail out BlockFi, this was an open question.

Is The Earn Model Over?

In the aftermath of the crisis, a key question many have asked is: Is the earn model dead? It seems likely the answer here is no, at least not completely dead. The more conservative companies in the space such as Ledn survived. Maple also survived relatively intact. Unchained Capital, which was even more conservative seemed to be almost completely unscathed by the crisis. The old 2018 Bitcoin as collateral thesis remains intact, some Bitcoin investors still want to borrow US Dollars to spend on houses and cars, while avoiding capital gains tax. At the time of writing, the platforms which did not suspend withdrawals are by and large still open and still offering decent interest rates. BlockFi for example is still open. However, the size of the balance sheets of these organisations has shrunk dramatically and it is unlikely we will see exponential growth again, at least for a few years.

What Happened to Do Kwon?

In September 2022, the Luna and UST founder Do Kwon had an Interpol Red notice issued against him. Kwon is said to have fled South Korea in the summer of 2022 and then moved to Singapore. However, after the Interpol notice was issued there were rumours Mr Kwon fled Singapore. His current location is unknown and he has refused to confirm his location. Mr Kwon is also questioning the legitimacy of the Interpol notice, arguing that cryptocurrency is not regulated in South Korea and the government had previously argued this themselves to improve its electability. Therefore, Kwon has said he believes the legal proceedings are politically motivated and implied he may not turn himself in in Korea, at least at this point in time.[168]

While Do did appear to behave in a reckless manner, it is perhaps not fair to blame him for the entire crisis. It is true Luna and UST collapse was the catalyst that set off a chain reaction, which caused a crypto-Lehman type moment, resulting in FTX stepping in as the lender of last resort, potentially preventing or delaying an even larger calamity. However, if it were not for this catalyst, something else may have come along and pricked the bubble. Do Kwon had the perfect character traits to succeed in the economic environment in that period. Do was confident, articulate, persuasive, ambitious, greedy, aggressive and narcissistic. There were many others like him who succeeded. When interest rates are set recklessly low and the system is awash with liquidity, money will pour into unstable and maniacal investment ideas. In a way, Do just adapted to the times.

---

[168] https://unchainedpodcast.com/do-kwon-of-terra-it-was-never-really-about-money-or-fame-or-success-ep-408/

17

Celsius

There is one major earn platform not covered in the previous chapters. One of the earn platforms was managed so poorly and ended in such calamity, that it deserves its own chapter. The company in question is Celsius. Celsius Network launched in 2017 and conducted an initial coin offering (ICO) in March 2018, raising US$50 million for its CEL token. Celsius' CEO/Chairman and co-founder Alex Mashinsky was also considered somewhat of a darling in parts of the investment community. In an August 2021 fluff piece in the Jerusalem Post, entitled "Meet Alex Mashinsky, everyone's white knight", it described Alex as "a man with a mission, a frontline fighter for consumer rights and the ultimate king of innovation".[169] The article also said.

> *Mashinsky has a passion for protecting the average Joe against large corporations, controlling industries and monolithic institutions. He asked himself why these businesses should serve as supposedly irreplaceable middlemen when a service can be offered directly to the user at little or no cost.*

The article also talked about Mashinsky's successful background in voice over internet protocol (VOIP) technologies and equipment. After taking on the established telecoms companies, now Mashinsky, famous for wearing a Celsius branded t-shirt with the text "Banks are not your friends",[170] appeared to have a new mission, taking on the

---

[169] https://www.jpost.com/jpost-tech/tech-talk-meet-alex-mashinsky-everyones-white-knight-677441
[170] https://www.cnbc.com/2022/06/13/crypto-lender-celsius-pauses-withdrawals-bitcoin-slides.html

banks. As the article put it: "Depositors put their money in banks to make profits, but it's the banks that are reaping all the benefits." Celsius also had a motto with a similar message: "Unbank yourself".[171] This narrative from Mashinsky is somewhat ironic, given the Celsius business model appeared to be a banking business model. The company took customer deposits and lent them out, just like banks. Celsius never embraced the non-custodial, revolutionary and transparent anti-bank model cryptocurrency can enable. Instead, it seemed to only adopt the anti-bank rhetoric. In August 2021, the Jerusalem Post article claimed Celsius had a balance sheet with an incredible US$20 billion in assets. This made Celsius perhaps the single largest player in the earn space.

In November 2021, Celsius raised US$750 million from investors, valuing the business at US$3.5 billion. The lead investor was Caisse de dépôt et placement du Québec, Quebec's US$300 billion pension fund manager, who invested US$150 million. At the time, Alex Mashinsky said that he expected the US$3.5 billion valuation to double or triple by 2022.[172]

In November 2021 Mashinsky engaged in a debate on Bitcoin with the well-known Bitcoin sceptic, gold advocate and economist Peter Schiff. The most significant comments in the heated debate are summarised below.

> ***Alex Mashinsky:*** *We have 1.5 million customers and they hold over US$25 billion worth of digital currency, mostly Bitcoin. We don't see much leverage in the system.*
>
> *…*
>
> ***Alex Mashinsky:*** *A new base [Bitcoin price] is established at US$45,000 to US$50,000 and you are*

---

[171] https://www.youtube.com/watch?v=coarCkU251w
[172] https://cointelegraph.com/news/celsius-expands-funding-round-to-750m-tips-7b-to-10b-valuation-in-2022

not going to see Bitcoin go below that for a variety of reasons.

...

Alex Mashinsky: *All exchanges disclose all the positions, they tell you how many people are long and how many are short. Part of how Celsius creates yield is by lending to these exchanges and institutions, who are putting on these long and short positions. We know exactly what the leverage is.*

...

Alex Mashinsky: Bitcoin pays dividends, Peter! Bitcoin pays dividends! Try Celsius. 6.2% dividends.

Peter Schiff: What do you do to generate income on that Bitcoin?

Alex Mashinsky: I am happy to spend an hour with you, educating to you how [we do it]

Peter Schiff: You are trading. You are taking a tremendous amount of risk. Bitcoin itself does not generate yield.

Alex Mashinsky: No. It does.

...

Peter Schiff: You must be taking a tremendous risk to generate those returns.

> ***Alex Mashinsky:*** *We don't take tremendous risk. It is an amazing opportunity for people to unbank themselves. Even your own son chose Bitcoin.*
>
> ...
>
> ***Alex Mashinsky:*** *Let's do this again in a year and take a look and see what happens.*[173]

Mashinsky revealed that by November 2021, Celsius had assets worth over US$25 billion. While it is possible Alex may have been exaggerating a bit, Celsius had reached an enormous scale incredibly quickly. In May 2019 the company only had US$200 million of assets.[174] Mashinsky also revealed excessive hubris and arrogance, especially about the Bitcoin price. Like Do Kwon, given the rampant speculation in the space, he appeared to be the right person for the time. In June 2021, the market capitalisation of the CEL token reached almost US$2 billion.

The following chart, which was obtained by extracting data from the eventual bankruptcy filing, shows that in some periods Celsius was consistently attracting over US$20 billion of gross inflows a month.

---

[173] https://www.youtube.com/watch?v=YaNXa4yLv-w
[174] https://pacer-documents.s3.amazonaws.com/115/312902/126122257414.pdf

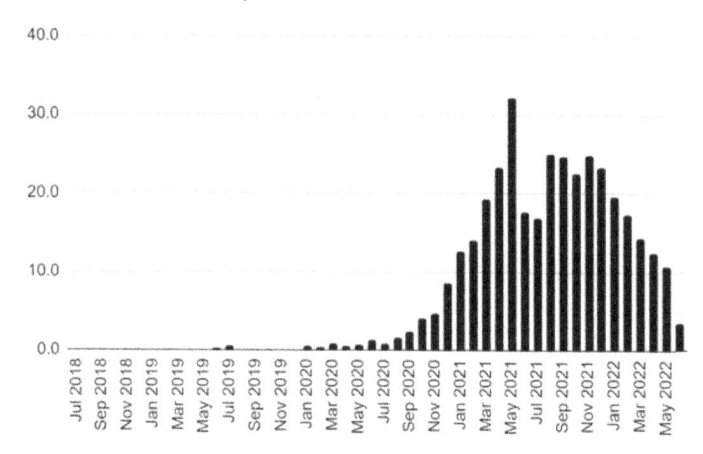

Celsius Gross Monthly Client Fund Inflow - US$ Billions

Source: https://pacer-documents.s3.amazonaws.com/115/312902/126122257414.pdf
Note: The information in the bankruptcy filing is somewhat unclear, therefore assumptions have been made in producing the above data, which could be incorrect.

The above data may be somewhat misleading, as it could contain flows from large professional counterparties who repeatedly moved money in and out. The next chart shows *net* monthly client flow and may be more useful. In some periods in 2021, Celsius was able to attract almost US$10 billion of net monthly inflow. Celsius was able to attract such large inflows due to its reckless, but also very attractive, interest rates. For US Dollar stablecoins, in June 2021, Celsius paid international customers 11.21%. In January 2022, the company paid customers a standard rate of 8.5%, which increased to 10.73% for "Platinum level" customers. This was at a time when BlockFi had lowered rates and introduced caps. In January 2022, the company paid Bitcoin deposits 7.81% on the first 0.25 Bitcoin and then 3.83% on balances above this. Celsius had perhaps the highest earn rates in the space.

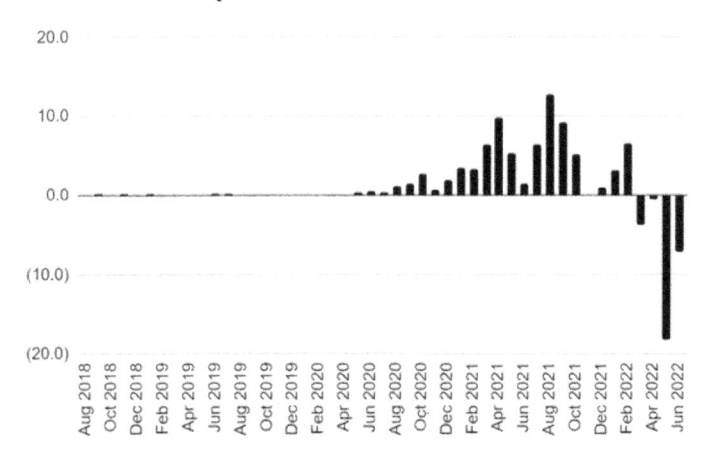

Celsius Net Monthly Client Fund Flow - US$ Billions

Source: https://pacer-documents.s3.amazonaws.com/115/312902/126122257414.pdf
Note: The information in the bankruptcy filing is somewhat unclear, therefore assumptions have been made in producing the above data, which could be incorrect.

Celsius was attracting huge flow, including from many small retail depositors. Celsius attracted so much capital that it appears as if the company was unable to effectively deploy it into solid investments. Celsius was awash with funds and there was not the capacity in the cryptocurrency space to conservatively deploy this volume of money. Therefore, rather than lowering deposit interest rates, the company may have taken inappropriate risks. Given the unrealistic confidence the CEO had shown with his Bitcoin price prediction, it is not that difficult to assume that some of Celsius' investments may have been a bit reckless.

Badger DAO Hack

In December 2021, Celsius admitted it lost US$120 million, in the BadgerDAO hack.[175] Badger appeared to be a DeFi based yield protocol of some kind, which we will not dig into here. On 2nd December 2021, the Badger smart contract experienced

---

[175] https://www.coindesk.com/markets/2021/12/03/crypto-lender-celsius-admits-losses-in-120m-badgerdao-hack/

"unauthorised withdrawals".[176] The next day it was revealed that Celsius was the victim. It is not clear why Celsius engaged with this smaller and less well known DeFi protocol nor was it clear if Celsius had the expertise to do so. This was a potential early warning sign of trouble to come. However, people in the cryptocurrency space have short memories and this incident was quickly forgotten.

Anchor Exposure

In May 2022, as the UST stablecoin failed, some raised concerns that Celsius may be exposed. According to a report from the industry specialist news organisation The Block, in an article published on 13th May 2022,[177] Celsius had significant exposure to Luna. The Block reported the following:

> *Crypto lending business Celsius had at least half a billion dollars of funds parked in Anchor Protocol but appears to have pulled all of it out over a frantic 24 hour period earlier this week.*

On 19th May 2022, Mashinsky addressed the concerns on Twitter. He denied there was significant exposure and accused people who were concerned of "trying to sell you competing services".

> *At @CelsiusNetwork we have stated several times publicly that we had minimal exposure to $Luna and $UST. I understand people who are trying to sell you competing services are spreading these rumours but you have to trust our @Twitter posts. Notwithstanding the extreme market volatility, Celsius has not experienced any significant losses and all funds are safe.[178]*

---

[176] https://twitter.com/BadgerDAO/status/1466263899498377218
[177] https://www.theblock.co/amp/post/146752/celsius-pulled-half-a-billion-dollars-out-of-anchor-protocol-amid-terra-chaos
[178] https://twitter.com/mashinsky/status/1527386747327418368

Suspension of Withdrawals

A month later, on 12th June 2022, a few days before rumours started circulating that 3AC was insolvent, panic was spreading in the industry and there were concerns raised about Celsius' solvency. Responding to accusations that Celsius may be in trouble, Mashinsky indicated that these concerns were "misinformation" and that those raising concerns may be taking "tradfi's" side.

> *Mike do you know even one person who has a problem withdrawing from Celsius?, why spread FUD and misinformation. If you are paid for this then let everyone know you are picking sides otherwise our job is to fight Tradfi together...[179]*

The very next day, on 13th June 2022, Celsius formally announced it was suspending withdrawals. Celsius used that same familiar language of other platforms, blaming "market conditions".

> *Due to extreme market conditions, today we are announcing that Celsius is pausing all withdrawals, Swap, and transfers between accounts. We are taking this action today to put Celsius in a better position to honour, over time, its withdrawal obligations.[180]*

In early July, while customers could not withdraw, Celsius paid down much of its DeFi debt. The company paid back 146 million USDC to AAVE and over 53 million Dai, withdrawing the Ethereum and Bitcoin it had as collateral.[181] The decision to pay back this debt, in the face of such a liquidity crisis, indicated to many that some DeFi platforms had better margining and collateral requirements than many of the centralised counterparties in the space. Had Celsius not done this, they could have been liquidated and perhaps lost more money. The smart contracts could not have treated Celsius any differently if

---

[179] https://twitter.com/Mashinsky/status/1535767334668861440
[180] https://celsiusnetwork.medium.com/a-memo-to-the-celsius-community-59532a06ecc6
[181] https://thedefiant.io/3ac-ghosts-everyone-celsius-fights-back

they were insolvent or bankrupt. To many, this highlighted the strength of these DeFi platforms.

Bankruptcy

A month after the suspension of withdrawals, on 14th July 2022, Celsius filed for bankruptcy protection in a highly revealing 61 page document. The document cited misleading media coverage as one of the reasons for the collapse, rather than focusing on mismanagement of the company.

> *As Celsius attempted to weather the "cryptopocalypse" storm, it began to receive increased negative media attention—a number of such stories were false and misleading. Immediately after the Luna collapse, social media spread misinformation regarding a commitment by Celsius and others to a possible Luna bailout, followed by statements that Celsius had lost hundreds of millions of dollars on Luna. These rumours made users wary of Celsius' platform and contributed to accelerated withdrawals of over $1 billion from the platform over five days in May 2022 at a time when distrust of cryptocurrency was at an all-time high*[182]

The document also included a balance sheet for the company, which indicated that the situation was worse than many had expected. The disclosure is provided in the following table.

---

[182] https://pacer-documents.s3.amazonaws.com/115/312902/126122257414.pdf

Celsius Network Balance Sheet As At 13 July 2022 – US$m

Liabilities	
User Liabilities	4,720
CEL Liabilities	210
Custody Liabilities	180
Other	390
Total Liabilities	**5,500**
Assets	
Bank Cash	170
Crypto Assets	1,750
Loans	930
Doubtful Accounts	(310)
Net Loans	**620**
Mining Assets	720
Custody Assets	180
CEL Token	600
Other	270
Total Assets	**4,310**
Deficit	**1,190**

Source: https://pacer-documents.s3.amazonaws.com/115/312902/126122257414.pdf

The disclosure shows a deficit of US$1,190 million, on assets of just US$4,310 million. This indicates that the deficit was remarkably high, at 27.6% of the assets. How the company managed to get itself into this devastating situation, so quickly, is quite remarkable. Especially considering the recent raise of US$750 million of equity.

The situation may have been even worse than the provisional balance sheet indicated. Included in the assets were US$600 million of its own CEL token, compared to US$210 million of CEL customer deposits. This US$390 million asset must be very difficult to liquidate. Surely the bankruptcy of the company would reduce the demand for the company's own token.

Then there was the US$720 million investment into Bitcoin mining. The documents indicated that the company had a very ambitious plans with regards to Bitcoin mining:

> *Currently Mining owns 80,850 rigs with 43,632 in operation, and prior to the Petition Date, had an investment plan to operate approximately 120,000 rigs by end of 2022.*

It seemed likely that much of this investment would also need to be written down, given challenges in the Bitcoin mining industry in 2022. Namely the falling Bitcoin price, rising high energy costs and the record and growing hashrate due to over investment in 2021. Indeed, by this point, the market value of the ASIC mining machines Celsius had invested in were plummeting. On 26th October 2022, the largest Bitcoin miner in America, Core Scientific, of whom Celsius was one of the largest customers, made the following announcement.

> *The Company's operating performance and liquidity have been severely impacted by the prolonged decrease in the price of bitcoin, the increase in electricity costs, the increase in the global bitcoin network hash rate and the litigation with Celsius*

> Network. As a result, management has been actively taking steps to decrease monthly costs, delay construction expenses, reduce and delay capital expenditures and increase hosting revenues. In addition, the Board has decided that the Company will not make payments coming due in late October and early November 2022 with respect to several of its equipment and other financings, including its two bridge promissory notes. As a result, the creditors under these debt facilities may exercise remedies following any applicable grace periods, including electing to accelerate the principal amount of such debt, suing the Company for nonpayment or taking action with respect to collateral, where applicable. Any such creditor actions may result in events of default under the Company's other indebtedness agreements.[183]

Given the above, it now seems likely that Celsius may have been somewhat optimistic in valuing its mining business at US$720 million. One can argue that such a large investment in a high-risk long duration asset like Bitcoin mining was not appropriate for a company with on demand deposits like Celsius. Nor is it the type of investments many customers may have wanted.

Further Accusations

In addition to the above, there were other accusations of wrongdoing against Celsius and the CEO Alex Mashinsky. For example, Alex is said to have withdrawn US$10 million from the platform personally, in May 2022, before customer accounts were frozen.[184] In July 2022 a lawsuit was filed against Celsius by a business partner KeyFi.[185]

---

[183] https://www.sec.gov/Archives/edgar/data/1839341/000119312522270236/d395956d8k.htm
[184] https://decrypt.co/111081/alex-mashinsky-withdrew-10m-%d1%81elsius-before-freezing-customer-accounts
[185] https://iapps.courts.state.ny.us/nyscef/ViewDocument?docIndex=RvF30Mz2IZW63s1mjjau2Q==

- The lawsuit alleges that Celsius had inappropriate internal accounting controls.
- The document accuses the company of improperly accounting for certain payments owed to customers, resulting in a US$200 million liability the company did not even understand how or why it owed.
- The lawsuit also alleges that Celsius may have lied about the cryptocurrency hedging strategy, claiming it was hedged when it was not.
- The lawsuit also appears to imply that Celsius was insolvent before suspending withdrawals, but still continued to offer high interest rates to attract customer deposits, to meet liquidity needs. The document calls this a "ponzi-scheme".

On 27th September 2022, Celsius' CEO, Alex Mashinsky, finally put forward his resignation, because his "continued role as CEO has become an increasing distraction."[186]

US Dollar Tether Connections

Two years before the suspension of withdrawals, in June 2020, Tether invested US$10 million into Celsius at a US$120 million valuation.[187] On 8th July 2022, Tether disclosed that it provided a loan to Celsius, which was over collateralised in Bitcoin.[188] The collateralisation rate was disclosed at 130%. Due to the over collateralisation, Tether indicated it was able to close the position without suffering any losses. The loan was believed to be for US$1 billion and paid an interest rate of 5% to 6%.[189]

At the time of the 2020 fundraising, Alex Mashinsky said:

> *The crypto community has only a few great projects and we are excited by the investment from Tether*

---

[186] https://www.businesswire.com/news/home/20220927005812/en/Celsius-Network-CEO-Submits-Letter-of-Resignation
[187] https://www.prnewswire.com/news-releases/celsius-network-secures-us10m-equity-raise-with-tether-as-lead-investor-301081105.html
[188] https://tether.to/en/tether-discloses-celsius-loan-liquidation-process
[189] https://www.coindesk.com/business/2021/10/07/tether-has-lent-1b-to-celsius-network-report/

> *International as it will help us deliver USDt-based services to all our users.*

The CFO of Tether, Giancarlo Devasini said:

> *We have worked with Celsius Network Limited since 2018. We found them to have the same passion and commitment to the crypto community that we have. We look forward to advancing our relationship together.*

Tether therefore appeared to have a strong relationship with Celsius, which lasted all the way from 2018 to 2022. Due to this relationship and Celsius' scale, Celsius may therefore have had the ability to redeem USDT for US Dollars in the banking system faster than some other entities. Some of Celsius' trading counterparties may then have been able to access Celsius' superior redemption process. This may explain the professional counterparties who were some of Celsius' largest creditors at the point of bankruptcy. For example, Pharos (A Lantern Ventures fund), which was the largest creditor and was owed US$81 million.[190]

Customer Information Published

In October 2022, the bankruptcy court published a 14,000 page document, which revealed the identities and transaction histories of all of the creditors, including small retail clients.[191] The one gigabyte database was then processed and the website celsiusnetworth.com was launched, which allowed the public to search across the database of all Celsius' clients.

In addition to losing customer funds, the Celsius calamity became even worse. Customers now experienced a significant degradation in their financial privacy. This is considered by some as antithetical to the values and ethos of Bitcoin and cryptocurrency.

---

[190] https://www.bloomberg.com/news/articles/2022-07-14/celsius-bankruptcy-filing-shows-long-reach-of-sam-bankman-fried
[191] https://news.bitcoin.com/bankruptcy-court-publishes-14000-pages-of-celsius-customer-usernames-and-trade-history/

Customer Loss Examples

The bankruptcy court received some written testimony from some of Celsius' clients. Some of these comments are summarised below.

> *I have more than US$30,000 of funds with Celsius which have been locked since June 12th 2022 which in turn brought me into [insurmountable] tax complications. I understand that a lot was shared, said and communicated to you already by many affected people regarding the misleading, fraudulent and deceiving business practises and the systemic misinformation and untruthfulness that was deeply rooted in Celsius' as a company which I can only echo. This, of course is besides Celsius' fundamental mismanagement and inadequate risk management which led to the loss of millions of dollars for their clients who trusted them with their retirement savings like myself.[192]*

> *I have elderly parents whom I care for and the assets currently held in Celsius [are intended] to help them live out their last years in comfort. I pray I will see my funds returned in full.*

> *I have a mental disorder and I cannot sleep now. I haven't slept since the account was frozen.*

> *Please jail these people, they are still getting crazy salaries from our money. [...] They have zero shame for what they did. They are evil and if you do not stop them, they [are] going to do it again and again to other people.*

---

[192] https://cases.stretto.com/public/x191/11749/PLEADINGS/1174908012280000000096.pdf

> *This has an immense impact on my life. I hope this can have a positive outcome, since a lot of people were victims to the deception of Mr. Mashinsky and his company.[193]*

To make things worse, not all the depositors thought they were buying risky cryptocurrency. Many of them just deposited in US Dollars and were not seeking upside exposure to high-risk cryptocurrencies, they just wanted to receive interest payments for US Dollar deposits. Many of these small depositors certainly did not want exposure into the somewhat rotten and hazardous world of the crypto credit system.

Celsius ended in a complete calamity, hundreds of thousands of ordinary people lost huge amounts of money, in many cases funds which were critical to them. These depositors had exposure to extreme risk, which they appeared to have been poorly informed about. Customers also had their privacy violated. The magnitude and consequences of Celsius' failure was appalling. With marketing and messages about being "for the people" and "against the banks", ironically, the company appears to have operated in a manner similar to that of the worst behaviour in the banks in the run up to the 2008 global financial crisis. And almost at a scale which matched that too.

---

[193] https://cryptonews.com/exclusives/anger-worry-doubt-celsius-customers-pray-for-return-of-their-crypto.htm

Part Three

Proof Of Stake

18

Proof Of Stake

In early 2011, seventeen year old Vitalik Buterin discovered Bitcoin. While sceptical at first, as the price of the coin increased, he began researching it, before covering the topic as a writer for Bitcoin Magazine. By Autumn 2013 he was already contemplating something called "Cryptocurrency 2.0". While with Bitcoin one could make financial payments, the idea was that the blockchain could be more flexible and support a whole plethora of features and applications. These ideas included distributed exchanges, domain name registries, messaging applications, gaming and more layers of tokens. It was possible to do much of this on Bitcoin, however some in the Bitcoin community were keen to only focus on financial payments. In addition to this, adding these layers of features on Bitcoin was technically very challenging, normal Bitcoin nodes wouldn't enforce the rules of these applications or each new type of application would require a specific upgrade to the Bitcoin network rules. It was not practical to build these systems on top of Bitcoin. The idea of Cryptocurrency 2.0, which was later named Ethereum, was that it would natively support any kind of application, enabling all kinds of innovative ideas that Vitalik hadn't even thought of yet.

Ethereum conducted a crowd sale in 2014, raising US$18 million worth of Bitcoin and the new blockchain finally launched in 2015. Right from the start Ethereum was always contrasted to Bitcoin, its ancestor system. However, almost every individual parameter and mechanism in Bitcoin was tweaked or improved for Ethereum. During the crowd sale Ethereum proponents made one thing clear, they eventually intended to use a different consensus system to

Bitcoin. While Bitcoin uses Proof of Work to select the valid blockchain to follow, Ethereum was going to move onto something called Proof of Stake. However, at the start, Ethereum was to use Proof of Work, until researchers could work out how to build a strong enough Proof of Stake system.

Proof of Work is a mechanism whereby computers perform a calculation called a hash function using the data inside the block as an input. These hash functions need to be conducted many millions of times, each time randomly changing part of the input, until randomly by chance, the output of this hash function is of low enough value. The more of these hash functions you do, the more blocks you are likely to produce. Conducting these hashes requires computational power, which requires electrical energy, a real world resource. This thereby anchors Bitcoin to the real world, the world of energy and industry. The valid chain with the most energy spent on it, is the one nodes follow.

Proof of Stake, on the other hand, is when nodes choose the blockchain with the most accumulated stake backing it. For this to work, stakers set coins aside in a pool and then bet, vote or attest to a particular block and the blockchain to follow is the one with the most votes. The chain still has hash functions, which prove the order of the blocks, by referencing the previous blocks, however there is no significant difficulty target. The output of the hashes can have any value in a pure Proof of Stake system, it does not need to be especially low. While Proof of Stake technology was not ready in 2014, Vitalik was determined to switch to it after further research into it had been conducted.

There were several major technical flaws in Proof of Stake systems, the most significant of them being something called the "Nothing at stake" problem. This is the idea that it is possible to maliciously use the same stake twice on conflicting competing chains. It was possible to punish stakers for doing this, but sometimes changing your mind and staking on two chains was totally legitimate, after all changing one's mind to follow the majority is how consensus is supposed to be achieved. Ethereum struggled with this problem for years. Eventually it was discovered that arranging stakers into committees helps mitigate the problem. Rather than all stakers having the opportunity to vote on each block, stakers were arranged into groups and only a tiny subset of the stakers were allowed to vote on each occasion. Thereby, individual stakers no longer need to change their minds, as if they made the wrong decision, a different set of stakers would be able to decide. By the time the staker had a chance to vote again, the "mistake" would already be part of history and decided on by others. There are still other outstanding technical issues and uncertainties with respect to Proof of Stake, however, eight years after Ethereum conducted the crowd sale, in September 2022, Ethereum finally switched to Proof of Stake.

One of the key reasons for switching to Proof of Stake is avoiding the environmental externality from Proof of Work. Proof of Stake systems have no anchor to the real world, it works entirely within itself. In a Proof of Work system, a significant proportion of the rewards are emitted externally, to semiconductor foundries and power producers, while in Proof of Stake, rewards are kept within the system. Therefore, while Proof of Work uses real world resources to secure the chain, Proof of Stake is said to be more efficient.

Some have pushed back on this idea, arguing that this logic, claiming Proof of Stake is more efficient, is economically flawed. The argument is that by using coins to stake, this capital is not being used for other productive purposes. For instance, perhaps one is delaying consumption or forgoing investment into productive assets. This may therefore be the inefficiency of Proof of Stake systems. Comparing the level of efficiency between Proof of Work systems and Proof of Stake systems may therefore be extremely difficult. The difference being that Proof of Stake obscures the waste, while Proof of Work does not. Perhaps, the first person to criticise Proof of Stake in this way is Paul Sztorc, in 2015.[194]

---

[194] https://www.truthcoin.info/blog/pow-cheapest/

There may be a reasonable analogy here with an argument made by the French economist Frederic Bastiat's in his 1850 essay on the "Parable of the broken window".[195] In Bastiat's essay a small boy breaks a pane of glass and the economic consequences of this are discussed. The same Bastiat who had argued in favour of the legitimacy of interest, in a debate with Proudhon a year earlier.

> *Suppose it cost six francs to repair the damage, and you say that the accident brings six francs to the glazier's trade – that it encourages that trade to the amount of six francs – I grant it; I have not a word to say against it; you reason justly. The glazier comes, performs his task, receives his six francs, rubs his hands, and, in his heart, blesses the careless child. All this is that which is seen.*
>
> *But if, on the other hand, you come to the conclusion, as is too often the case, that it is a good thing to break windows, that it causes money to circulate, and that the encouragement of industry in general will be the result of it, you will oblige me to call out, "Stop there! Your theory is confined to that which is seen; it takes no account of that which is not seen."*
>
> *It is not seen that as our shopkeeper has spent six francs upon one thing, he cannot spend them upon another. It is not seen that if he had not had a window to replace, he would, perhaps, have replaced his old shoes, or added another book to his library. In short, he would have employed his six francs in some way, which this accident has prevented.*

Perhaps the environmental cost of Proof of Work mining is easier to see, while the delayed consumption or forgone capital investment,

---

[195] https://en.wikisource.org/wiki/Essays_on_Political_Economy/That_Which_Is_Seen,_and_That_Which_Is_Not_Seen

associated with large investment inflows into Ethereum, attracted by the staking yields, will go unseen. The logic here is somewhat controversial. It seems perhaps almost impossible that we will get universal agreement on these apparent costs of Proof of Stake, just like we can't agree on whether central banks keeping rates too low for too long caused the economic boom bust cycles. Can we really get all these economic benefits for free? Be it an unstoppable distributed consensus system or strong sustainable economic growth and continued asset price appreciation, or is there always some unseen hidden cost that eventually emerges in the form of a crisis?

Some supporters of Proof of Stake systems have argued that Paul Sztorc's logic is flawed, because capital may only be locked up for a short amount of time. In Ethereum, at the time of writing, the funds are actually locked up in staking and cannot be withdrawn at all, until the network upgrades. However, once this upgrade occurs, one should be able to withdraw the funds within perhaps a few months, depending on several factors such as the length of the exit queue. Other alternative Proof of Stake systems allow even faster withdrawals, within a few weeks. Therefore, supporters of these Proof of Stake systems argue, nothing is locked up and there are no externalities. Paul Sztorc has a retort to even this, in any competitive system, he asserts, marginal costs will tend to marginal revenue. In other words, if there are rewards for staking, people will keep spending more and more costs to earn those rewards, until profit margins are low, no matter what those costs are. Anyway, even if the funds are not locked up, as long as they are deployed in a staking protocol, they are not used to invest in productive projects.

Ethereum switching to Proof of Stake or "The Merge" as it is called, is a significant development for the cryptocurrency space. One potential consequence is that it could attract many new yield hungry investors. The high yield could make Ethereum a more attractive asset to hold, boosting the price. It could also be said to make Ethereum even more speculative. Even though the Merge has often been cited as positive for the price of Ethereum, as the coin's supply growth may be more constrained than under Proof of Work, the positive impact the yield could have on the price may be underestimated. Switching to Proof of Stake is also assumed to boost the appeal of Ethereum to environmental, social and governance (ESG) minded investors, who may be worried about investing in Bitcoin due to the perceived high carbon footprint of Proof of Work. Although this environmental argument may attract investor flow into Ethereum, it also may not have as significant an impact as the yield.

Ethereum's native yield could cause a huge flow of funds into Ethereum, from outside the cryptocurrency world. Of course, there are other Proof of Stake coins, however outside investors are perhaps correctly sceptical of these other high yields, wondering where the yield comes from. Ethereum has far greater legitimacy than these other coins and a much more powerful marketing infrastructure and more real users. The Ethereum developers are also smarter than the developers of the other Proof of Stake coins and they have therefore designed a stronger system, one which is more resilient. The combination of these factors could send the price of Ethereum to stratospheric levels in some of the future cycles.

19

The Proof Of Stake Interest Rate

The yield one earns when staking Ethereum is in some ways similar to an interest rate. Of course, it is not technically an interest rate, in that it is not formed as the result of a credit relationship, however it does result in a passive income stream. The staking yield is also counterparty risk free, like the lightning network rate in Bitcoin. However, Ethereum staking is much more passive and the scale of this activity is much larger, making the Ethereum staking yield economically significant. While staking, there is the risk of getting hacked as the private key needs to be on an online machine. On the other hand, stakers can have a separate withdrawal key and staking key, protecting their funds to some extent, as only the staking key needs to be kept on the online machine. However, an attacker could always submit malicious votes with the staking key, which could cause most of the coins to be lost.

Ethereum staking launched in December 2020. However, at the time the staking network was somewhat of an experiment and not used as the consensus system for Ethereum, it was a separate blockchain running in parallel to the main Ethereum chain. However, you could still use "real" Ethereum and earn real Ethereum from staking in the experimental network. In September 2022, the Merge occurred. This meant that the staking network was used as Ethereum's consensus system, and it was no longer an experiment or test system. However, coins can still not be withdrawn from the staking network and this feature is expected to be added in a year or so.

At the end of October 2022, around 14.6 million Ethereum was staking.[196] These funds were worth around US$22.9 billion. This represented around 12% of the outstanding Ethereum supply. The variable yield obtained by the stakers in late October 2022 is around 5.5%, based on the average rate over the previous month.

When staking launched in December 2020, the yield was around 13%. This higher rate was needed to attract deposits into the staking contract. As more deposits came in, the rate gradually declined, until the late summer of 2022, when the yield reached a low of 4.5%. Since then, after the Merge, the rate has climbed up moderately, to the 5.5% level. Although the yield had these gradual trends, on a day-to-day basis the rate can be quite volatile as network conditions change, however the rate is reasonably stable across several weeks. This 5.5% rate is quite high for an asset like Ethereum and is likely to attract the attention of many investors.

Staking Yield Algorithm

The precise yield one earns from staking Ethereum is determined by a number of factors. It can be influenced by part of the transaction fees users pay, the tips, as well as staking network conditions such as the participation rate of the stakers and the staking performance. The full details of the factors that determine the yield will not be covered in this book. Most of the mechanisms which determine the yield are designed to try and ensure the highly complex staking system achieves the consensus needed to keep Ethereum working. Therefore, economic considerations do not seem to be the primary concern of the designers when these parameters were set.

However, by far the most important principle determining the yield is the number of coins staking and this can be considered an economic factor. The key consideration is that the amount of newly issued Ethereum which is awarded to stakers is approximately proportional to the square root of the number of coins that are staking. Therefore,

---
[196] https://beaconcha.in/

the fewer coins are staking the higher the staking yield and vice versa, according to this quadratic relationship.

This can be thought of as a stability mechanism. If yields in DeFi become more attractive, driving stakers away and into DeFi, the staking yield will climb in a quadratic fashion. The yield will eventually get so high that the outflow of capital ceases. On the other hand, if the DeFi yield opportunities are poor and there is a flow of Ethereum into staking, the yield will decline. A high yield would no longer be necessary to attract stakers and a yield too high could result in too much Ethereum unnecessarily being issued, which could cause the price of Ethereum to decline. Therefore, as more people stake, the staking yield declines.

It is not yet clear if the number of coins staking will change with the economic cycle. For instance, if falling US Dollar rates will push investors to purchase Ethereum and start staking. Alternatively, rising US Dollar interest rates could cause stakers to leave. The history only shows the number of staking coins increase, as this is all the protocol allows at the moment. Technically, the protocol does allow stakers to exit, however, if this occurs now, the coins are trapped in a kind of limbo, therefore for all intents and purposes, until the network upgrades, the staking balance is only likely to increase.

The cryptocurrency cycle could also impact the number of coins staking. In booming times, the number of coins staking could be low, as investors are instead earning high yields providing liquidity in DeFi and obtaining more exposure to Ethereum using leverage. Then the economic cycle could turn. With fewer opportunities available, more coins could start staking, which is a relatively safe activity compared to engaging in leverage and the staking yield could then decline.

On the other hand, the above is mostly speculation and the impact of a bull or bear market on the number of coins being staked is not clear. There is no precedent here. An alternative idea is that a bear market crash could see people needing liquidity. Therefore, the number of coins at stake could decline, as people need unstaked Ethereum. After the liquidity crunch is over, coins could return and stake again.

Ethereum Supply

When considering the staking yield and the issuance of new Ethereum to compensate these investors, it is important to consider the Ethereum supply. While newly issued Ethereum is created and allocated to stakers, this does not mean the Ethereum supply will get out of control. The maximum inflation rate, if almost everyone stakes and stakes perfectly is only around 1.6% per annum or about two million coins per annum.

1.6% is therefore the lowest rate a staker should ever expect to earn. If this yield is too low that shouldn't be a problem, because everyone is already staking. On the other hand, if this 1.6% level is too high, too many coins may stake and there could be a problem. Guaranteeing a yield of at least 1.6%, across economic cycles, does potentially seem a bit unsustainable for a potentially appreciating currency and this could be a small risk. However, it may be necessary, as network security needs to be funded.

Ethereum has also implemented a transaction fee policy where a significant proportion of the transaction fees are burnt, which can reduce the supply of Ethereum. Therefore, if demand to use the Ethereum network is high, despite the newly issued coins and staking yield, Ethereum could be a deflationary currency.

20

Staking Derivatives

One of the most well-known potential weaknesses of Proof of Stake systems is the existence of staking derivatives. There is also the wider concept of simply outsourcing the staking process. This is when an Ethereum investor sends their Ethereum to a third party, who conducts staking on their behalf. This outsourced staking is potentially a serious problem with regards to the security and effectiveness of the staking consensus system. These third-party staking intermediaries take custody of the stake and the risk here is therefore potentially far greater than when Proof of Work miners use mining pools, as the usage of pools does not result in a change of control of the physical mining power.

The outsourcing of the staking process feels almost like a mainstream financial product, for both retail and institutional investors. Staking can economically be considered as a process which is purely financial in nature. Unlike Proof of Work mining, which can be thought of as an industrial process. As long as this industrial process continues, Bitcoin should continue to survive.

Most of the large cryptocurrency exchanges either offer or plan to offer custodial staking services. At the same time, staking seems quite suitable for an investment product. Why should anyone invest in a plain vanilla Ethereum fund or exchange traded product when they could invest in a version with staking and earn a higher return? Of course, many people actually need to use Ethereum to pay gas fees and balances needed for this cannot be staked, however most holders of Ethereum are still speculators and investors. For these investors they are likely to want staking investment products.

Core to an effective staking protocol is the slashing mechanism, a system whereby stakers are punished for bad behaviour, such as changing their vote and attempting to conduct double spend attacks. If staking is outsourced, the operators of the staking servers do not own the underlying stake and therefore they may not be sufficiently deterred by the slashing punishment system. Although, you could argue a similar problem occurs in Proof of Work, where ownership of the miners and operation of the miners could be separated, for example when a public company engages in Bitcoin mining.

Outsourcing the stake can also cause centralisation, if staking is concentrated in the hands of a small number of players. This could eventually result in the network being vulnerable to censorship and then the utility of Ethereum could quickly degrade. Financial products which pay a passive yield are often prone to the pressures of centralisation. The investment and financial services industry has a track record of consolidation and winners scooping up all the capital, often more so than in other industries. Regulation and economies of scale are a key driver for this. The centralisation here could be worse than in Proof of Work, where the natural geographic dispersion of appropriate energy assets, across multiple jurisdictions, could protect the system from centralisation to some extent.

This centralisation is already a significant problem in Ethereum. Based on data from beaconcha.in, the top five staking services already account for 60.7% of the network by stake. These services are often cryptocurrency exchanges, who do not own the underlying coins and are staking on behalf of their customers. These exchanges typically already have relationships with financial regulators and a service like staking, which pays a yield, could very well be seen as a regulated financial product. Therefore, the risk of regulation and censorship is very real, even in the medium term.

Staking Service	Percent of stakers
Lido	28.2%
Coinbase	12.9%
Kraken	7.8%
Binance	5.9%
Staked.us	5.9%
Other	39.3%
Total	**100.0%**

Source: https://beaconcha.in/pools#distribution

Due to some of the nuances in the protocol, the impact of this possible censorship is difficult to assess. Proof of Stake is a far more complex system than Proof of Work and therefore discussing how the network may be censored can be quite difficult. We will not go into the details here, but a possible outcome is that many of these services stop providing staking services or reduce the extent of their services and provide a degraded yield. The result of these staking services ending or coming under intense regulatory pressure could be the following:

- Limited actual effective censorship,
- A slower blockchain in periods of turmoil related to the censorship,
- Eventually, a more diverse staking landscape, with better censorship resistance characteristics,
- Fewer stakers,
- A lower Ethereum price, and
- Higher staking yields.

Tokenised Staking Derivatives

The entities performing the outsourced staking as a service business, could also issue tokens to their clients, representing shares in the staking pool. Staking rewards could then be issued to these token holders. These new tokens could be issued on top of the Ethereum blockchain. The coins would be just like Ethereum, except they have credit risk associated with the staking pools and you cannot pay gas fees with the coins.

There are several key advantages associated with these token products. They provide owners of the staking pool the ability to enter and exit more easily, by buying or selling the tokens, without any lags. The tokenised staking coins also mitigate another key potential problem associated with staking on Ethereum. The staking yield needs to compete with other yields inside the Ethereum system, for example yields you could earn by providing liquidity in DeFi. With this tokenised staking approach, stakers can now earn two yields at the same time, thereby partially negating this problem. For example, one could deploy the staking pool token into the DeFi ecosystem and earn even more yield. These staking tokens could even have basically all the key properties of Ethereum. You could use them to make payments, make markets and even use them as collateral to borrow other coins. This also can be said to solve the other problem with proof of stake systems. The staking tokens, in theory, could even be invested in productive projects or spent on consumer goods. Therefore, no funds are locked up and no useful investments are prevented due to Ethereum's staking system. With these strong and clear advantages, it is even possible that almost all the staked coins end up in tokenised staking derivative pools. Therefore, pretty much all the economic problems with the staking protocol could be solved.

The above may sound too good to be true and it probably is. There must be a catch somewhere. We can't have all these advantages and no real costs. This very much exposes an ideological difference that various commentators and analysts in the cryptocurrency space have when evaluating Proof of Stake systems. Some people believe that you can't have something for nothing and look for weaknesses. They believe that if it appears as if you have something for nothing, this may persist for a while, but the system will be unsustainable and eventually fail, perhaps in a catastrophic crisis. Others, a more optimistic group, do believe a consensus system with no real costs is possible and are actively trying to construct one.

The flaw in their reasoning, that staking tokens solve all the economic problems, appears to be that many of the security assumptions on which the Proof of Stake consensus systems relies, may begin to break down. If everyone has staking tokens and uses them for a variety of functions, such as making payments, providing liquidity in DEXs or as collateral to borrow, the ultimate economic beneficiary of the tokens will not be the same entity as the entities which are staking. Therefore, the actual stakers may not be sufficiently compensated by the rewards in the staking system, or sufficiently threatened by the punishments in the system. This issue, of misaligned incentives is quite common in the investment industry. Another issue is that if everyone is staking, then perhaps there is no real staking yield at all. If the yield is paid to everyone, then it looks more like adding zeros on to the end of the currency than a genuine investment return. It would all be smoke and mirrors. This system could work for a while, perhaps many years, but eventually it could result in a catastrophic failure in consensus. The multi-layered staking system could then collapse.

Despite this potential weakness, staking derivative tokens have proved to be extremely successful so far. There are three main providers of these tokens. Lido has stETH, Binance has bETH and Rocket Pool has rETH. At the time of writing, Lido is in the lead and the stETH token has more Ethereum backing it than the two other tokens, which are small by comparison. A potential problem here is that this could be a winner takes it all type market. The economies of scale in tokens are extremely high. For example, the network effects when making and receiving payments are large and tokens with stronger liquidity on offer on exchanges can become dominant. Therefore, the centralisation risk is high and this is a considerable issue for Ethereum.

stETH

Around 28% of the staked Ethereum is currently allocated to the Lido pool and exists in the form of stETH. This is about US$7.2 billion worth of stETH floating around, at the time of writing. The most liquid venue for buying and selling stETH, is on the Curve DeFi exchange protocol.

In theory, the price of stETH should always be less than or equal to the price of Ethereum, because one can always subscribe for more stETH at par, by adding Ethereum to the Lido staking pool. One cannot yet redeem stETH for Ethereum, as stakers cannot yet withdraw. Therefore, for now, stETH should trade at a small discount. Once the withdrawal feature is implemented and activated, stETH should track the price of Ethereum more closely and its utility should therefore improve. This may result in the creation of even more stETH. Before the upgrade, stETH should trade at a discount, reflecting the uncertainty as to whether this upgrade occurs and when it occurs.

One key part of the June 2022 earn crisis left out of this book until now is stETH. Many of the earn platforms, like Celsius and trading counterparties, such as 3AC, had invested in stETH to earn the yield. However, their liabilities associated with this were typically in Ethereum, not stETH. Therefore, when the liquidity crisis occurred in June 2022, they had to pay back their clients in Ethereum, but they only had stETH. The trouble is of course that stETH is not redeemable. Therefore, the earn platforms had a significant duration mismatch.

Therefore, there was a rush to sell stETH on Curve. A significant stETH discount of around 3% first emerged in mid May 2022, as

Luna failed. Then, during the peak of the crisis, on 18th June 2022, stETH traded as low at 0.925 Ethereum. Finally, by the end of September 2022, the price of stETH recovered, to a discount below 1%. 3AC received a significant haircut when it liquidated its stETH in the crisis.[197] On 14th June 2022, 3AC sold 30,000 stETH.[198] Celsius is believed to have held US$426 million of stETH, making it perhaps the largest holder.[199] Again, Celsius is likely to have taken a considerable haircut.

Remember, Curve is not like a traditional exchange with an order book. Curve operates the Ethereum vs stETH market with two pools of liquidity, an stETH pool and an Ethereum pool. With all the pressure to sell stETH in May and June 2022, the pools became unbalanced. For example, in mid June, the pool had around five times as much stETH as it did Ethereum, 500,000 stETH and 100,000 Ethereum. One may think such an imbalance would cause more of a price dislocation than just 7.5%. However, Curve has a custom shaped curve with special parameters for each trading pair. Since the stETH vs Ethereum pair was designed when people expected the prices to be reasonably similar, the curve shape prevented the discount from reaching even larger levels. This benefited some of the distressed entities such as 3AC and Celsius. As we went into July 2022, some people wanted to buy stETH at a discount and eventually the pools became balanced again. At the time of writing the breakdown is 50.3% stETH and 49.7% Ethereum.

What the earn collapse showed, was that in a liquidity crisis, people preferred Ethereum to stETH. This was at least the case in this crisis. In the future, if the stETH ecosystem is more developed, people may be happy holding stETH as a form of liquidity in a crisis. In addition to this, an stETH crisis is unlikely to repeat itself in the same way, because next time there is a major cryptocurrency liquidity crunch Ethereum may have upgraded and stETH may be redeemable. On the

---

[197] https://www.bloomberg.com/news/articles/2022-06-15/crypto-hedge-fund-s-cryptic-tweet-fuels-speculation-over-losses
[198] https://etherscan.io/tx/0xe115178f496b3d016a1cc37917ebaf3642efa30512cc67137520c3a9bbf29ce7
[199] https://www.coindesk.com/markets/2022/07/12/celsius-reclaims-410m-of-steth-tokens-after-paying-down-81m-debt-to-aave/

other hand, even after the upgrade, there will be limits on the number of stakers who are allowed to withdraw in any given period. If all the stakers try to withdraw at once, the process could take over a year. Therefore, some kind of liquidity crisis causing a race to exit staking is possible, with the staking tokens trading at a discount.

Interest Rate Swaps

Another very different potential form of a staking yield derivative is an interest rate swap. With this type of product an investor could lock in the Ethereum yield for a period of time, converting it into a fixed income type product. For example, a staker could purchase a swap contract entitling them to receive fixed payments and pay variable payments, based on the actual Ethereum staking yield. This investor would then have locked in their staking yield at a fixed rate. They would no longer need to worry about more stakers joining or fewer miner tips causing the yield to fall. This swap type interest rate product is very popular in traditional finance. These fixed income type products can be attractive for certain investors, who for example, may have fixed liabilities they need to cover, for instance somebody who has borrowed Ethereum at a fixed rate. On the other hand, if someone has lent out Ethereum, they may be concerned the yield could increase and they could take the other side of this swap trade.

These swap products do not seem to exist yet. As the cryptocurrency economy becomes more accustomed to Ethereum's inherent variable yield, it seems likely that many financial and derivative products may emerge that enable traders to speculate on, fix or hedge the important quasi-interest rate.

21

Proof Of Stake Economy

Once the staking yield establishes itself in the Ethereum economy, the yield could begin to act like a risk free rate in Ethereum or an Ethereum base rate. In theory, nobody should lend Ethereum to anyone at a rate lower than this rate. Why should anyone make a risky loan, if they could earn the same or higher rates earning yield in this counterparty risk free way? Therefore, the staking yield could provide a floor to other Ethereum based interest rates.

If the staking yield is too high, it could prevent or "crowd out" other loans denominated in Ethereum or other Ethereum denominated DeFi yield generating products. It could make loans or other DeFi yield generating activity economically non-viable. This may be a disappointment to many in the Ethereum community and would represent the manifestation of a risk identified in 2015 by Paul Sztorc. At the time this problem was considered as only a theoretical weakness. However, it may one day have practical ramifications. This weakness could be mitigated by modifying the protocol and lowering the yield. Afterall, the algorithms which determine the yield rates were made up, it's possible the wrong parameters were set and they may need tweaking. Tweaking the parameters could be challenging, as there could be a delicate balancing act between preventing the crowding out of other yield generating use cases and ensuring enough coins are used in staking to secure the network.

The staking yield could also influence and drive other lending rates or other DeFi related rates, just like how the base US Dollar rate drives other rates in the economy. The staking yield could eventually act as a kind of benchmark rate, with some loans contracted at a rate which is a fixed spread over the staking yield rate. This is similar to the traditional banking system, where some people have variable rate mortgages, which follow the central bank base rate plus a fixed spread. DeFi smart contracts could reference the staking yield, factoring it into its calculations or using it as a benchmark to determine other rates. For example, AAVE could offer a new product, quoting a spread over the staking yield rate to those who want to borrow Ethereum. OTC lending companies like Genesis could contract with proprietary trading firms, to lend out Ethereum at the staking yield plus 2%, for example.

Proof of Stake is complicated enough at the technical level. As the last part of this book explains, Proof of Stake and the associated yield is also quite complex when analysed using an economic framework. Determining the economic endgame for Ethereum's Proof of Stake system is therefore difficult. It's possible that stETH becomes more dominant, resulting in an increasingly centralised and unstable system. Under the surface there is the pretence of a Proof of Stake system, but in reality, it barely matters, with most investors engaging with stETH.

The centralisation pressures on highly financialised systems like staking do seem quite considerable and therefore Proof of Stake systems may be too exposed to centralisation risks. The system could therefore be exposed to the risk of a regulatory crackdown. This seems like a possible potential outcome and therefore investors should be weary.

Ethereum's staking system is a financial system and it therefore should be analysed using a financial and economic framework and it may be exposed to financial risks. Financial systems often contain imbalances that can build up over the years behind the scenes. Imbalances that only become apparent in a crisis. Proof of Stake systems could also be susceptible to this type of risk. Afterall, the staking system has no anchor to the real world; it just operates on its own. There is an analogy here to the fiat money standard, after gold convertibility closed in the 1970s, the financial system also lost its anchor to the real world. There was nothing to keep the system in check and extreme imbalances could build up, resulting in a potentially unstable system. Likewise, Ethereum's consensus system no longer has an anchor to the real world, the Merge can therefore be contrasted to the removal of gold convertibility for the US Dollar in 1971. Ethereum could therefore become more vulnerable to dislocation and extremities. There will never be universal agreement as to whether the removal of this anchor was a good idea or not, just like some economists today still blame many of our economic problems on structural imbalances which have built up over time due to the lack of an anchor in the financial system. These economists do not believe in a world where you can keep lowering interest rates to keep everyone happy, eventually there will be costs. Proudhon's dream was not realistic and using analogous logic, Proof of Stake can't survive forever either, it's too good to be true.

The effectiveness of the staking system could therefore degrade over time, with the weaknesses and financial imbalances not apparent until it's too late. It therefore seems possible that the system may one day fail or almost fail. However, the pathway to this potential failure or what it may look like is not clear. It could be a change in the economic climate that causes the calamity, resulting in a panic flow of funds out of the staking system. On the other hand, the protocol does have systems in place to deal with this, such as an exit queue and this risk may seem somewhat farfetched. DeFi proved the critics wrong in the way it handled the crashes in May 2021 and June 2022, and the Proof of Stake system could also prove itself to be more resilient than many of the critics think.

It is possible that Ethereum is extremely successful for many years and enjoys considerable price appreciation, with the staking system making a material contribution to this success. If you like excitement, volatility and rapid price appreciation, Ethereum and its staking system are probably for you. Ethereum's Proof of Stake system could have many years left in it. If you prefer resilience and something that you can have confidence in to withstand the worst forms of economic and financial chaos, Bitcoin and its Proof of Work system is probably your best bet. The Proof of Work system may well survive longer than the Proof of Stake alternative.

Made in United States
North Haven, CT
12 November 2022